CHAMPAGNE SALARY:

DIARY of a TOKYO HOSTESS

ROSE BEACH

PEGASUS BOOKS

www.pegasusbooks.net
First Edition: May 2012

Published in North America by Pegasus Books. For information, please contact Pegasus Books c/o Ms. McGhee, P.O. Box 235, Neptune, New Jersey, 07754.

Champagne Salary: Diary of a Tokyo Hostess/Rose Beach – 1st ed

ISBN 978-0-9832608-5-1

1. BIO026000 BIOGRAPHY & AUTOBIOGRAPHY/Personal Memoirs. 2. OCC019000 SOCIAL SCIENCE/Inspiration & Personal Growth. 3. SOC022000 SOCIAL SCIENCE/Popular Culture. 4. TRV003050 TRAVEL/Asia/Japan. 5. TRV001000 TRAVEL/ Special Interest/Adventure. I. Title.

10 9 8 7 6 5 4 3 2 1

Comments about *Champagne Salary: Diary of a Tokyo Hostess* and requests for additional copies, book club rates and author speaking appearances may be addressed to Rose Beach or Pegasus Books c/o Ms. McGhee, P.O. Box 235, Neptune, New Jersey, 07754, or you can send your comments and requests via e-mail to rosebeach13@yahoo.ca

Also available as an eBook from Internet retailers and from Pegasus Books

Printed in the United States of America

Some names have been changed to protect the privacy of individuals.

To all the strong and inspiring women I met in Roppongi,

You helped me see the beauty and humor of each situation and that true and lasting friendship exists.

HER CHAMPAGNE SALARY WOULD BE ENOUGH TO MAKE HER DREAMS COME TRUE. OR WOULD IT?

Raised on a small farm in the rural northwest, Rose Beach grows frustrated with waitressing and struggling to earn money for college and a music career. When a friend tells her about the hostessing industry in Tokyo, where pretty western girls can earn huge salaries for lighting cigarettes, pouring drinks and singing *karaoke* in clubs, Rose decides to take a chance.

Champagne Salary is Rose Beach's personal account of her introduction to the Japanese hostess industry, including the myth and the reality. Sharing a tiny apartment with five other women in Roppongi, she is immersed in the world of Tokyo nightclubs where she, along with her new friends, deal with dress codes, curfews and strict expectations from club managers.

 Within the clubs, she meets many colorful characters, develops friendships, risks danger and discovers love.
Along the way, Rose is transformed by Tokyo and returns to Canada with a new strength and perspective about her own life.

Champagne Salary is written in a casual, warm style, like a friend sharing selected scenes from her diary. At times it is informative, funny, shocking and sad, but always entertaining. It is a book you will want to share with friends!

CHAMPAGNE SALARY:

DIARY of a TOKYO HOSTESS

by Rose Beach

Edited by Caprice De Luca

Champagne Salary:

Diary of a Tokyo Hostess

by Rose Beach

HARD WORKING GIRL FROM A SMALL CANADIAN TOWN

I grew up in a town of two-thousand people, in an environment of strength and integrity, in a family of strong, confident women. I was stimulated, but I was bored. I had just been fired by another power tripping restaurant manager from yet another grueling job as a waitress and I felt I had no way out. I was broke as a joke.

When I was younger, I fantasized about being a waitress. My large, inquisitive eyes would widen as I stared at the smiling servers who brought platters of steaming delicious food and bowls of vanilla ice cream, smothered in hot fudge. I thought that the staff was lucky beyond belief.

I still smile remembering the feeling of euphoria after I got a job as a waitress in our town's only Chinese restaurant. After my first shift, I drove home with a feeling of success and a pocket full of tips. They were well appreciated, as I was an eager young woman with material needs and a family that couldn't afford them.

Growing up in the only Métis family in a bigoted farming town, my family faced many challenges. We were the working poor. My earliest childhood memories were of dancing around my mother as she busked in front of the liquor store for a few dollars so that we could have dinner. By that time she had three kids under five to support. Times were tough, but we danced around in the bitter cold, not even feeling its bite.

My granny grew up during the time of Indian Agents, when Canadian aboriginal children were scooped from communities and sent to live in the residential schools. She and our grandfather were taken from their homes and sent to a place where they were forbidden to speak their language and study their culture. The government's policies were of assimilation and First Nations people were considered inferior. Instead of receiving love and kindness, they were dehumanized and abused.

That injustice would lead to many unhealthy communities within First Nations societies and would negatively impact generations to come. When they came of age, they broke free from the residential school's control, but they were ill-equipped to support themselves and deal with the horrific memories that would haunt them for the rest of their lives.

They fell into addictions to escape their pasts. My granny spent time in jail and was no stranger to prostitution. The jailhouse tattoos she tried to cover were a grim reminder of that past. But she was a caring mother when she was sober and a great cook who would invite any and all of the town's homeless over for Thanksgiving dinner. In later years, she managed to pull herself from a downward spiral and was a strong advocate against child abuse and hard drugs.

My mother remembered her mother's soft, gentle hands when my grandmother brushed her hair and told her how beautiful she was. With the confidence she instilled, my mother was able to break the cycle of abuse. Even though my mom had a rough life, she never forgot that her mother loved her.

Before my mom met my stepdad, I never remember having a nice room of my own. I shared a bedroom with my younger brother and twin sister. The only thing that belonged to me was a foam mattress I used for sleeping. And though we didn't have any toys or material possessions, we seemed to keep each other entertained by making up plays and songs and chasing each other around.

My mom would play music at the old age centers, and we would work for weeks to perfect shows with elaborate thrift-store costumes. We would always be hungry when we got to the old folks homes and we often fantasized about the kind of yummy sweets that might be on display.

Even after my mom married my stepdad and our lives changed for the better, we were not well off financially. When I was a little girl, material things were the least of my concerns, but as I got older, I started to crave possessions and money to buy them. That meant I needed to work.

At first, I loved waitressing and the money that it put in my pocket to do with what I wanted. My friends would come in and we would chat about all the things that were important to teenage girls, like boys and clothes. But at the end of high school came a time of great pressure and hard choices about the path toward my future and career.

I had always enjoyed school and excelled at it, but I had more than just a thirst for knowledge. I wanted to be a musician. Even though I was hesitant to admit it, I had to be honest with myself about what I felt.

I had already studied classical and jazz trumpet throughout school and found it fulfilling, but I wanted more. I longed to write and sing my own music, and to do that I would probably need a life lesson or two. So I decided to throw myself into the world and just go with the flow.

I knew there was a one in a million chance for me to succeed in the music industry, but I couldn't help but enjoy the desire that burned deep within me whenever I thought of becoming a true artist. I considered my mother an authentic artist since she was not afraid to bare her complete soul on stage, no matter who might have been standing in judgement, and there were many.

The Chinese restaurant I had worked at turned out to be a dream job in terms of bosses. They had always been nice to me no matter how late I was or how many plates of chop suey I spilled. But my lucky streak was about to end.

The day I graduated high school, I left my small town for good. With my sweetheart beside me, we hightailed it out of town in a pick-up truck with what modest belongings we had. We both got jobs in a place that was as breathtaking as it was unforgiving.

Eventually the steep cliffs that enclosed the gorgeous valley where we slept every night in each other's arms started to close in on us. One source of stress was my getting fired from various jobs. I couldn't keep a job for longer than a couple months and it was starting to affect my self-esteem and my relationship with my boyfriend.

I hadn't planned on serving in a fast paced, stressful work environment. During those days I was constantly on edge and nervous about making a mistake. The repercussion I faced for messing up someone's order was dealing with the wrath of the management and the kitchen. I had a string of unkind managers in the previous few months, but I found myself being scrutinized by the worst ever.

"When you're done with your section's prep work, you can go help Marie finish up on toilet duty." The manager's whiny voice was a lesson in patience. Every day after my shift, I gave a symbolic high five for not throttling my manager, Marvin.

I tried to feel sorry for him because he was unattractive and he lacked social skills. He was the kind of guy who loved to talk just to hear the sound of his own voice. His braces would flash as he regaled us with stories about mountain climbing, his only hobby (besides jerking off!). Marvin made it near impossible to like him, but that didn't stop me from trying to find some good in this man who was really just self-conscious.

I adjusted my tight red T-shirt with the bar's logo and attempted to hike up the plunging neckline so that the customers weren't so googly-eyed when I bent down to clear the tables. They weren't paying me enough for that. The smell of the burgers cooking on the massive grills in the kitchen made me queasy and I prayed that my boyfriend's condoms were working and I was not pregnant.

I tried to hide my pasty face with a forced grin as I nodded toward Marvin while clearing the tables in my section. The tips of the white squeeze bottles on each table were always congealed with dried up black ketchup. I liked to clean those rank little bottles. Next to wiping the crumbs off the seat, it was the most satisfying part of my day.

Marvin liked to watch me as I prepared for my shift so he could point out the flaws in my cleaning. He would stop me by grabbing my hand and directing it to the proper area. It was infuriating. I had only been working there two months, but I could already feel my patience wearing thin. I tried to meditate and be positive, remembering that I was lucky to have the job.

I supposed when he fired me at the end of the night for not getting my orders out fast enough I should have been relieved. I don't know why I cried behind the steering wheel of my pick-up truck, but I did. I felt the shame of failure as my cheeks grew hot. "It's just not working out," he had told me with a mixture of authority and pity.

There was no way I would ever put myself through that again. I would have rather died than break my promise. I looked at my tear-stained, puffy face in the mirror and tried not to feel sorry for myself.

"Today is the first day of the rest of your life," I resolved, wiping away my tears. At least he had not seen me cry. I did not want to give him the satisfaction. But I was scared about my future.

I had few options with no post-secondary education. I did not want to get a student loan and go back to school for something I was not passionate about. But on the other hand, I sure didn't want to keep on going the way I was going.

I needed to make money in order to have time to write and develop myself as an artist so that I could record a CD. Making an actual CD seemed like such a pipe dream though, a fantasy really.

I had been writing music with my mom and performing with her. I loved the feeling of being on stage and having someone listen to our message. But the more I looked around the more I saw struggling artists, scrambling to make ends meet. It took a very strong person to live that life and I did not know if that was me.

My twin sister was forever asking me to come to Vancouver and live with her. In a struggling relationship with my man, I was tempted to take her up on her offer. But one day she dropped a bombshell on me, telling me she was pregnant. I was not surprised when she told me because I had a dream about her baby the night before.

As twins, we were extremely close since birth. When we were infants and they tried to separate us, we cried until they moved our cribs together. I always knew when something was happening to her, good or bad. We fought like cats and dogs, but we loved each other more than words could say.

I missed her every day and dreamt about her often. So the day after I was fired from the last waitress job I would ever have, I packed my bags, kissed my boyfriend goodbye forever and drove west, toward Vancouver. After a few nights of partying and catching up with my sister, I decided to get serious about my future.

With each passing day I was feeling more and more like a sailor. When I saw the ocean for the first time, it was if I had found a long lost friend. I would stare out across the open, slate-colored water for hours, wishing for the opportunity to cross it. My chance to travel came from an unlikely source.

When my twin and I reconnected with a girlfriend in Vancouver, she told us all about being a hostess in Japan. I was immediately intrigued. My ears perked up at the mention of traveling to Asia.

Hooking up with a local hostess agency was easy, as she had gotten offers left, right and center for contracts. Her name was Barbie, and she was gorgeous, with bleach blonde hair, a curvaceous body and a perfect face, due to plastic surgery.

She had a bubbly, charismatic personality and we loved spending time with her. She often told us tales of *karaoke* singing, champagne and fancy, frivolous gifts. Girls had been known to get houses, cars and diamonds from special customers. They made great salaries and had all their expenses paid.

To our delight, she loved to retell the story of one customer who upon finding her admiring his Mercedes tossed her the keys and insisted that she accept it as a gift. She later sold it for over fifty thousand dollars.

Still, the idea of being a hostess just did not sit well with me. I wondered why normal men would pay to talk to a woman. There had to be some sort of hanky-panky going on. I did not want to get myself involved with that kind of work. I had always listened with great interest, but also with a lingering wariness.

It wasn't just the potentially seedy job that made me nervous. I had never been out of Canada. I was twenty-three years old and I had never even seen the ocean before visiting my twin in Vancouver, let alone crossed one. Half of me felt excited, the other half felt just plain scared.

And I had never considered Tokyo, not with an actual plan to go there. The thought of it was surreal, as if it did not exist. Strange, cartoon-like images popped up and jumbled in my curious mind. I expected stereotypical things like ninjas, geishas, and Harajuku fashion.

I thought I would probably be surrounded by a country full of geniuses and robots. And while I was sure I could buy an "Inspector Gadget" utility vest, I was more excited about searching for vending machines filled with everything from dirty underwear to wasabi ice cream.

After I made my decision to bite the bullet and accept a hostess contract, I held a plane ticket in my shaking hand with a mixture of overwhelming anticipation and complete terror. Even though I was intrigued, I was terrified to travel to such a foreign country alone and work in such an obscure and intimidating industry.

But empty bank accounts do not lie. It was either do or die and I did not plan on dying in another waitress job. My creativity was stifled and I needed a change of scenery. Plus, I intended to keep my promise.

That solemn and calming vow became a mantra. It played over and over in my mind like a broken record. "Today is the first day of the rest of my life," I repeated as I took a deep breath and steeled myself for what was next.

My future employer paid for my airfare and accommodations, so all I really needed when I left Vancouver was a few clothes. After I checked my suitcase in, I bolted over to the bathroom so I could cry in peace in the stall of that empty airport restroom. I missed my twin already and I needed to release the pent-up emotions that were threatening to consume me.

NARITA

I felt the tires skip onto the tarmac of the airport and was jolted awake. I was still groggy from the eight hour booze fest of a flight from Vancouver to Tokyo. My head was pounding. Japan Airlines had plied me with mini bottles of red wine and Japanese beer. Every time I turned around, I was getting an *oshibori* and a drink.

It was the first time that I had flown internationally, so I expected bad service and even worse food. But I was surprised by the excellent dinner and polite staff. They really knew how to treat a passenger.

"Don't mind if I do," I smiled and took another mini bottle from the friendly air steward. "Cheers! How do you say that in Japanese? *Kampai?*" I was proud of the first Japanese words I could utter besides *Domo arigato, Mr. Roboto.*

The flight was worth the experience. I had a noticeable red wine mouth that I tried to scrub away, squeezed into the airplane bathroom, engaged in a last ditch attempt to appear somewhat respectable.

I had a distinct sense that I reeked of airplane alcohol and debauchery. Debauchery, that's right – something not to be expected from a goat milking, girl-next-door type farm girl. I was a nonconformist, but I had been known to milk the occasional goat.

I was calm as I approached the immigration counter with a ready red wine smile and a quarter pound of vacuum packed premium BC bud, hidden in my lucky pink and white polka dot panties. In my defense, the date was almost 4/20 and I was planning a three month stint in Japan, during which time I had a responsibility to satisfy my enormous *ganja* habit.

Most people would have been nervous, but my brain would not entertain fear or paranoia, regarding both as futile. Barbie told me that weed was beyond expensive in Japan, and I just did not have the cash to spare. Besides, I was not about to go hunt it down in a foreign, megalopolis, not when I did not even speak the language.

¥10,000 was pronounced ten thousand yen. I would soon be so familiar with the currency that I began referring to ¥10,000 as an *ichiman*. That was about one hundred dollars, and that was also the price of the tiniest baggie of weed in Tokyo. I was not down with the idea that I might have to start conserving and rolling toothpick-sized doobies, not when I was used to the luxury of free smoke in Canada. My family *grew their own stone*.

After I sailed through customs, I was on a smuggler's high. It was the first time I had ever smuggled, but the thrill of getting away with it produced a high that was better than having the drug itself. Customs did not even look at my suitcase.

I was hoping I was not going to have a secondary problem, because I had packed pepper spray. Before I left, my mom had insisted that I take it for protection. She had not wanted me to go at all and was paranoid about my safety.

My granny always told my mom never to do two illegal things at once. So there I was, smuggling weed, pepper spray and about to start working illegally. I hoped it was not a bad omen, but I refused to allow myself negative thoughts on such a happy and momentous day.

I breathed a sigh of relief upon exiting into the "Arrivals" area. I had finally gotten my luggage cart to work for me, after realizing I had to push down on the lever to get it to go anywhere. I had a five minute battle with it before one kind woman took pity on me and showed me the secret.

The airport was industrial and air conditioned, but my surroundings seemed neon after such a long flight. The jet lag made everything appear as if in slow motion. I vaguely remembered the pilot telling us it was late afternoon, but I could not see any sunlight anywhere to betray his statement.

The airport in Vancouver was modern and full of First Nations art. It was a marvel of architecture and design. But the airport in Narita held no charm. In fact, it was almost scary.

I could not see anyone who was looking for me and the only contact I had for the club was a well-worn piece of paper with a cell phone number scrawled on it in faded ink. I looked around for a payphone, eventually realizing that I did not have any Japanese coins for a call. Just making a phone call in this foreign country would be a huge undertaking.

I turned to my left in an attempt to locate the person who was supposed to meet me and I noticed an overweight, half Japanese man in a polyester suit. He made his way over to me with a purposeful stride. His eyes were as small as pinpricks and his complexion was so youthful that I could not get a sense of how old he was. He could have been twenty, or fifty.

He fixed his gaze on me, nearing, and when he finally reached me he only spoke one word through a heavy accent, "Jennifer?" I nodded my head, and that was good enough for him. We were off without a word of explanation or introduction.

I wondered how he had found me so quickly, but as I looked around, I saw a sea of Japanese faces. I was a head taller than most of them, with platinum hair and shades. I stuck out like a sore thumb.

I saw an odd, red-faced, European man and a backpacking tourist, but mostly it was Asian men in business suits and older, petite ladies, wearing large hats and traveling in chattering groups. I followed my guide outside and was blown away by a wave of heat, the likes of which I had never felt before.

"Are you Mikey?" I asked, hoping to strike up a conversation. One of the only pieces of information I got before I left was the name of the club. He nodded his head with pride, and in a seeming afterthought, he ogled me up and down, like I was a piece of meat.

I shoved my first impression to the side and smiled at him as we waited in line for tickets. It appeared he did not understand much English. I imagined his English was as lacking as my Japanese was.

We boarded the "limousine shuttle," which turned out to be a disappointment because it was just a bus, nothing fancy. As we rode the one and a half hour ride into Tokyo, Mikey started dozing off (I would eventually realize that people slept literally everywhere and anywhere in Japan). Actually, I was glad to be in my own company, and as we approached the famous Rainbow Bridge, I caught my first glimpse of night-time Tokyo.

Something inside me changed in that instant. I had never seen anything so spectacular. The twinkle of the lights dazzled my retinas and the enormous buildings lining the vast coastline made me feel like Alice in Wonderland. The Rainbow Bridge stretched as far as the eye could see. I was in awe of all that surrounded it.

Cranes and ships dotted the shoreline as we passed enormous buildings and rows of tiny apartments. Each unit's windows reflected a separate shining color from the kaleidoscope of signs that hung everywhere. The closer we got to the center of Tokyo, the more impressive the architecture got. On one side I saw a huge chrome dome structure, which Mikey said, mumbling, was a TV station.

After we crossed the bridge and I saw Tokyo Tower, I experienced *déjà vu*. Yet before I could explore that feeling, we were immersed in wall to wall traffic, giving me the slightest sense of just how many people there were in Tokyo.

There were construction workers, dressed in baggy pants that reminded me of Super Mario Brothers. They drove in tiny trucks next to men in cars who talked on cell phones. The executives drove cars that cost more than most people's annual salary. No matter what the mode of transportation, the masses were swarming around all at once, trying to get somewhere.

On every corner there were rows upon rows of people, waiting to cross the street. There were brightly lit restaurants and hair salons with women getting updos, as they painted their faces and eyelashes. The ever present neon lights serenaded my senses and the imposing buildings seemed to heighten my awareness of everything Japanese and foreign.

Pulling up in front of the ANA Intercontinental Hotel in Akasaka was like a dream, and for a moment I imagined myself robe clad, enjoying gourmet meals delivered by room service. But I suspected my destiny would be far less spectacular than residing in a five-star hotel. As we stood on the sidewalk, the hotel porters hailed us a taxi. As I slid into the cab, I allowed myself one last glimpse of luxury before beginning the taxi ride to my new home.

Funny fact about the taxis in Japan – the doors open automatically for you, but only on the left hand side. When I sat down, I was surprised to find that the seats have enormous white doilies on them, and the driver wore starched, immaculate, white Mickey Mouse gloves.

The stoic taxi driver flew down the curvy, narrow roads at unthinkable speeds. The streets sped by, flagged by signs with Japanese characters that to me were marvelous. I had no idea what the signs meant, but I did not care, because the calligraphic bold black writing on every sign captivated me.

When Mikey and the driver began to speak in Japanese, I finally perceived how different this world would be. I suddenly felt very alone and out of place. And worse, I had no idea about the job that I was about to begin. All I really knew was that I had been contracted out to a club to be a hostess. I was becoming more apprehensive by the minute.

According to Barbie and others I spoke with, being a hostess was not the same as being a call girl, like everyone in Canada and most other Western countries thought. It was an acceptable and necessary job in Japan, where hostesses were required to pour drinks, light cigarettes, sing the occasional *karaoke* song and basically provide good company.

I supposed it to be something like being a modern day imported *geisha*, except that *geishas* were highly trained and skilled, while I didn't know what the fuck I was doing. I made the resolution to fly by the seat of my pants. Besides, I was in Tokyo. I had arrived.

AZABU TOWERS

Mikey asked the driver to stop, and we pulled over in front of a non-descript grey apartment complex, boasting the only English words in the nearby vicinity, *AZABU TOWERS*. It was situated among condensed, packed rows of almost identical buildings.

I was disappointed with what I had seen of Tokyo architecture in this area of the city. I had expected glitz and glamor or extremely high-tech security and hologram technology. When I glimpsed a Wendy's and a McDonald's, I felt deceived because I had expected sushi and kimonos. I had a lot to learn about Japanese culture.

I had reminded myself to write down the address, so that if I ventured out, I would not get lost. Mikey carried my bags to a decades old elevator, and after a short, creaking ride, he showed me to my shabby room. My future employer had not sprung for any extra perks on my account. Mikey mimed that he would come back later.

As I inspected my surroundings, I decided to be stealth and deposit my weed sack in my suitcase. I could have my celebratory smoke after checking for signs of roommates. There were two other bedrooms, so I guessed I was not alone. It was fine with me, because I loved company.

I missed my sister terribly, and I felt even worse for leaving her alone and pregnant in Vancouver with very little income. I wanted to be there for her because she had split up with the father and she did not have a huge support system. I decided I would send money back to her as soon as I earned some. On the plane ride over, I made a decision to find a "pseudo twin" among the girls who would be working with me.

Stepping into that communal space would have been claustrophobic for some. Fortunately, I had always felt comfortable in small places, which no doubt came from sharing a womb. The main entryway was adorned by a huge clock which Mikey patted, as if to remind me that the time had changed.

The main room was used as a kitchen, living room and bathroom, all in one. The kitchen to the left consisted of a small sink with a black faucet, a Bunsen burner and a microwave, sitting atop a miniature fridge that may have been white at one time. I paced the room in a few easy strides and placed my luggage in the room Mikey had indicated would be mine.

There were three doors leading to three separate bedrooms. I had to duck to get into my room because the doorframe was so low. My room contained a bunk bed, a bare clothes rack and a mirror, hanging from a wall with peeling wallpaper.

As I entered the main room, I could not help but stare at the airplane sized bathroom situated almost in the middle of the room. The only color was provided by the avalanche of cosmetics that littered the entire room. Makeup, blow driers, deodorant and stockings covered the space, without an apparent trace of food.

I glanced at the clock on the wall and saw that it was almost seven p.m. Tokyo time. Calculating, I realized that it was one a.m. in Canada, meaning I had somehow lost a night. I would have to make up for that.

First things first, I had to set up my iPod and speakers. But just as I was about to crank Tanya Stephens, a gorgeous Amazon of a woman entered the room in a G-string and wife-beater, obviously having just rolled out of bed. She stretched toward the ceiling yawning, her mouth wide open. She had high cheekbones and an unruly mop of short, platinum hair. She was the most stunning woman I had ever seen.

"You a new girl? You want some soap?" she said.

"Pardon?" I asked, wondering if she was suggesting I smelled bad.

"Soap," she replied slowly, like I was a dummy. "I make it."

"You can make *soap*?" I asked, impressed.

"Of course! Anybody can," she scoffed.

And with that last comment, she proceeded to add hot water from a kettle into a bowl containing a package of corn *soup*. I had misunderstood her accent, and obviously "soap" meant *soup*. I would have been blown away if she had been making that soap on the stove by candlelight.

She handed me the soup with gusto and stated in an offhand way, "They're gonna make you work tonight."

"Oh, no. No, I just arrived," I tried to explain.

"I know this, but get ready to work. I leave in one hour. I show you way to club. I'm Natasha." She did not offer me her hand.

"I'm Jennifer. What should I wear?" I asked, the only question that came to mind.

"Something sexy," she insisted, shrugging. And with that she finished her *soap* and exited to one of the rooms.

I decided to take her advice and get ready for work. After all, it was why I had come. Sure enough, Mikey came by later and seemed pleased that I was getting ready for work.

TITS AND LEGS
AKA: MY FIRST NIGHT

I have great legs. It's a gift, and I am not so modest about them. In fact, I do not believe I have ever been called modest in my life. I also have great cleavage. I have been known to work *what my mamma gave me*, a nice body and a striking unusual face.

I loved getting dressed up. So I picked my most devilish outfit, a black, sequinned mini skirt and a "barely there" matching top with huge silver hoop earrings and thigh high black patent leather boots. With my long, blonde hair, I created quite a sexy look. I looked fine, and I was surprised to feel so energetic in spite of being awake for so long. I realized I was running on adrenaline, but I was ready to find out about the world of being a hostess.

Natasha hurried into the miniature kitchen, wearing city shorts and an elegant black silk top. She was easily six feet tall without heels on and there she was wearing four-inch stilettos that made her shapely legs look as if they went up to her neck. Through the silk of her top, I could not help but notice her amazing figure. Her big, sky blue eyes pierced through me as she searched her oversized, white leather bag for her sunglasses. Though it was already dark, she put them on as we walked down the street together.

We were dressed in very different styles. I looked like a *hoochie mamma* next to her, in the sleek, stylish outfit she had chosen. It was awkward. She was the one who had told me to dress sexy. When she noticed my apparel, she moistened her pink glossy lips.

"Police notice us less if we don't dress like hostess on street. I have hostess dress in my bag," she explained with her rolling Eastern European accent.

"Is being a hostess illegal?" I queried. I knew I was working illegally, but that was because I was there on a tourist passport and therefore unable to work. I thought the actual occupation was legal there.

"No," Natasha answered, "but we don't have working visas. Clubs get raided and girls go to jail for that. Always keep passport with you. If police stop you, they are looking for overstay visas. You will be okay. You have Canadian passport."

She began overloading me with information and my head started to spin as we walked out the door into the warm night breeze. I did not know what her last comment meant, but I was glad for any information, no matter how vague. I wished she had shared the "dress stealth" counsel earlier, but whatever. Beggars can't be choosers.

At that point, Natasha was my only friend in that unfamiliar new world. I grabbed my passport and followed her curvaceous frame out the door. On the walk to work, I noticed Natasha was not a very talkative person. She gave me monotone, monosyllabic answers that left me feeling uneasy.

"Where are you from?" I asked.

"Russia." The way she rolled her *r* sounded exotic.

"Cool. That must be an interesting place to live!" I sighed, trying to start a conversation, but she was not having it. "How many girls work in the club?" I tried again.

"Twenty, maybe," she shrugged, stoic.

At that point I began to feel she thought she was doing me a huge favor by even talking to me. I did not enjoy it, so I ended the conversation and mentally checked Natasha off my pseudo twin list. According to the zombie walking with me, there were twenty girls in the club. One of them had to be my future pseudo and partner in crime. That cheered me up.

It was hot and humid outside. It was windy too, but the draft seemed to make me even hotter. I looked up, knowing that even though the sky was not overcast, I would not be seeing any stars in Tokyo. The smog was too thick and the city lights were too bright.

I pushed that lonely feeling away and focussed on the passing buildings and the groups of people milling around in front of them, talking in high-pitched excited tones. It did not matter if it was a thin business women dressed in grey, a tired business man or a group of school kids ready for action, I sensed a level of excitement. There was energy in the air that everyone seemed to share.

I was beginning to sweat, though I wore no jacket. As I surveyed the scene, I became aware there were cars everywhere, coming dangerously close to me. It was obvious that pedestrians did not enjoy the right-of-way in Tokyo.

There were smells wafting from all angles. The blasting vent of a Japanese restaurant assaulted me just as the smell of the vendors selling skewered meat crossed my path. I was already starting to feel sick to my stomach, but those new smells were making it a million times worse. The air was sticky with pollution, and every few hundred metres I would come across strong "fart zones," a.k.a. *the smell of a thousand asses,* emanating from the sewer.

The only time Natasha acknowledged me was to glance at me in a shared second of horror whenever we came across a stinky patch. I was in love with the experience, so in my mind the abhorrent odor gave it a kind of charm.

The stroll to work had suddenly changed. Grey apartment buildings gave way to upscale structures and quaint restaurants. Attractive couples sauntered along the tree lined streets. It felt like we were in Paris, not Tokyo.

As we continued walking the scenery changed, yet again. Now we were surrounded by flashing lights, and a variety of clubs. There were men lining the streets, handing out fliers for strip clubs and aggressively promoting discos. No one was exempt from their persistence.

Investment bankers, army boys, clusters of giggling Japanese schoolgirls and psychos, all bumped around together on the packed streets in front of me. You would never know who would turn out to be a mafia boss, an assassin, a billionaire or a poser.

I noticed almost everyone was dressed well, and I was aware of the power they exuded. I spotted a very tall, platinum haired woman, immaculately dressed, towering over and towing along a tiny, hobbling Japanese man who was laden with shopping bags. He wore a huge grin, as if to proclaim to the world, "I'm the man!"

There were people everywhere, and the air was charged with an infectious party fever. Suddenly, I realized where I was. I was in Roppongi.

Barbie had told me about Roppongi. She said it was one of the biggest and most multicultural party places in Tokyo. From her stories, the nightlife was supposed to be "out of this world," and many clubs stayed open all night. She told me many a tale involving the notorious Roppongi, so I was thrilled to finally be walking its legendary streets.

However, my excitement came with a sense of uneasiness that increased with every step we took closer to the club. I basically knew nothing of what would be expected of me. All I knew about a hostess club was it was usually frequented by wealthy, influential men who came to talk, sing and cavort with women from all over the world. That didn't explain a lot to me.

My biggest fear was I wouldn't be treated well by my employers or by the customers. I worried how I would deal in such situations. I tried to picture myself lighting cigarettes and pouring drinks, but I was falling short of my usual standards of imagination.

Another apprehension was my shyness about approaching men. I would never have had the courage to approach a man and ask for a date. I did not know how it would play out. I reconsidered my decision.

I wondered: *Would I be introduced to customers and what would I talk about? How long would customers stay? Would other girls sit at the same table? What was the appeal of paying for conversation?*

There were a million questions flitting through my mind as we arrived, a neon sign flashing in front. For the first time, I saw the name of the club, "Mikey's." I had expected something with a little more imagination.

Natasha pushed the button for the fifth floor and I looked around the minging elevator at the list of clubs. Most clubs had Japanese names written in *kanji* characters, which might as well have been an alien directory for all I understood of it. Some had just plain gross names like "Lips" while other clubs had funny names like "Bad Girls."

The tiny elevator was packed with hostesses and at each floor the doors would open to allow girls off. There must have been thousands of clubs in Roppongi if that whole nine story building contained clubs. I had not realized that there were that many hostesses in Roppongi.

As always, I had complete faith in my newest endeavor, but as the doors opened I could not help but feel a bit let down. The club was garish. A worn, red banquette wrapped around the entire room with matching smaller couches and seats set up to accommodate about forty people maximum.

The carpet was old to say the least, and it was covered with indiscernible patches of stain. There was a glass divider down the middle, over which hung a disco ball next to a large *karaoke* television. Random, impersonal feline art adorned the walls with gilded frames.

There was an enormous flower arrangement in one of the corners next to a table piled with whiskey, brandy and green bottles with mysterious writing on the sides. I would soon find out it was *shochu*, Japanese hooch made from rice, wheat or potatoes.

There were no customers. I had expected the scene to be more like Norm's bar entrance on *Cheers*. A warm welcome would have been nice as I walked into the raucous party while the patrons screamed "Jennifer!" rather than "Norm!"

"You better clock in," a voice insisted.

That brought me back down to earth. Natasha was changing next to me, not shy about flashing me her boobs in the miniature room we were all expected to get ready in.

"Go show Mikey your nails and get your stocking on. We have to get checked and clock in by 8:15." She gestured toward a time clock. A slow chill traveled down my spine.

Nails, stockings, time clock? Barbie had forgotten to mention those things. I had serious authority issues already. And I hated wearing stockings! I was horrified. Mikey entered the room to critique what we were wearing. He had a bored Japanese waiter with him, who looked about twenty-five. The waiter was handsome, but he had huge hair.

As Mikey spoke to him in brisk Japanese, the only words I understood were my name and "boots." I had expected maybe, "Welcome to Mikey's. Thanks for working under such short notice." I had quickly come to understand that any expectation I had about the industry should be forgotten immediately. After Mikey had finished his longwinded explanation, the waiter that he spoke to turned to me and said, "No boots."

I tried not to glare at the bored waiter as I kept my confrontational feelings at bay. I had vowed to myself that I would at least give it one night. The blind faith I had earlier was somehow failing me.

I steeled myself and bit my tongue as I watched yet another person try and dictate my life. I had left the world of waitressing so that I could get away from that fake feeling of control, and there it was slapping me in the face with its persistence again. I created a new mantra while listening to him and I had it on repeat in my head, "Breathe."

He droned on and on about the rules of the club. The absurdity of what he was saying made me want to interject so many times, but again I remained silent and tried to stay with my breath. It was really an exercise in meditation to listen to his crap and try to remain *Zen*.

"You need high heel shoe that goes around your ankle," he said. "No black. Except if you have *dohan*. Start tomorrow, always your nails polished and manicure."

I looked down at my hands, suddenly self-conscious. I had literally been on horseback the day before I left, so the thought of painting my nails had never even occurred to me. I had no idea what a *dohan* was, but I was sure I would find out soon enough.

"We weigh you now. If you get four kilograms when you are here you be fined ¥10,000." He paused there and waited like he was waiting for fireworks to erupt. When I was again silent, he breathed a little sigh of relief and quickly continued before I could protest a rule that objectified a continually thin woman as the ideal epitome of beauty.

"There is meeting every day at 8:15. Clock in after you are checked by 8:15 or you get penalty of ¥1,000 (ten dollars) every fifteen minutes. We open is 8:30. *Dohan* time is 9:00. No smoking." I would find a way around that. I deemed myself a chronic weed smoker, who was dedicated to doing it whenever I pleased. There was no way that I wasn't going to get my smoke on while I was here. That would be the place that I needed my medicine the most.

"You have to change name. We already have Jennifer from Ireland." The statement caught me off-guard. I have to admit, I took some offense, but still I said nothing. He expected me to change my name as easily as I changed a dirty shirt.

"We close is three a.m. You have curfew phone call at five a.m. to your apartment. You have penalty of ¥50,000 (five hundred dollars) if you miss that call. No boys in room or you be sent home." I really hoped that was the last rule because I did not know if I could remain silent for much longer. The club really knew how to put a damper on a girl's spirit. I had wanted to get my groove on in Japan and sample all it had to offer, including the men.

"Make sure that you have lighter with you and keep filling the customer drink before they are empty. Do you have passport with you?" Thank God it seemed like he was almost finished spouting off about all the things that I was forbidden to do. His speech made me want to break the rules all that much more.

The waiter gestured to a rack with various bright colored atrocities, which resembled dresses. I hesitated, wondering if he expected me to change into such unflattering clothing. If I didn't know any better, I would have thought they were trying to make it harder for me to adjust to my chosen foreign surroundings.

The new nickname that I immediately came up with for the waiter allowed me to find some humor in my situation, a tactic that always made me feel better. "Huge Hair" handed me a cell phone and said, "You must rent phone from the club."

Mikey flashed me a smile that was too bright and exited. I was not comfortable changing in the small office. I was finding it hard to hold onto my peace of mind. I wanted to quit right there. I had always had authority issues, but that was appalling.

Many people would ask me later why I didn't just walk out that door then and there, but I had few options. I was in a strange country, where I doubted that I could even find it home by myself, let alone find my way back to my country. Even though the urge to quit was almost stronger than I could handle, I had made a promise to myself.

I would have rather suffered that than experience the monotony and helplessness of being a waitress. I could give it one night. One night was not so much to ask. If I wasn't more optimistic by morning, I would find a way back to Canada.

So I put on a frilly, outdated monstrosity of a yellow dress that I would not have wished on my worst enemy. I wore that, along with white, patent leather shoes that had been on another woman's smelly feet, and a tight pair of white pantyhose. I thought I looked like Big Bird.

I then allowed myself to be weighed as I chose my new identity: Rose. I had always loved the name. Not only did it sound romantic, it had been my granny's name. In adopting my new name, I had taken on a new identity as *femme fatale* and I planned on acting the part well. I even chose a new last name. I would be known as Rose Beach.

I had a new plan too. I would work at Mikey's for one month, in which time I would: a) make as many friends as possible; b) make a shitload of money, and c) find a club to work at that did not have so many strict regulations. Judging from the number of hostess clubs that I had seen in the nearby vicinity, "c" wouldn't be that difficult.

That new plan made me feel more in control of the situation as I was ushered over to what appeared to be the waiting area and what I would later learn was called the "Dog Box." I got no introduction and quickly learned that I would have to get over my shyness and make the first move if I was going to thrive in the industry.

There were five other girls in the Dog Box, all possessing a Harlequin romance look. There were two girls in the waiting area sitting off to the left with Natasha. One had a brilliant red bob and another had long, curly auburn hair. They all looked similar, elegant and gorgeous, with pale white skin and cold eyes, as they spoke rapidly in a language I assumed was Russian. I caught a flash of familiarity in the blue eyes of the auburn-haired girl, but in the same second it was gone, replaced by a stone mask. I wondered if I could have imagined it.

On the right sat two girls in animated conversation. I was relieved to hear they were speaking English. They had great tans and wore funky mini dresses with plunging necklines. The one in pink was tall and lean, with sandy blonde hair. She wore it pinned up with a white flower behind her ear. The smaller girl had a dark, exotic look and was fairly jumping out of her chair with excitement. Her playful black eyes twinkled as she tossed her long black hair and smiled, displaying dimples. I decided to introduce myself.

"Hi everyone, I'm Je... I'm Rose." I would have to get used to my new moniker.

"I'm Anna," announced the redhead.

"I'm Svetlana," answered the shy auburn haired girl with a heavy accent. Then they went back to their conversation.

"I'm Diamond," replied the cute dark haired girl with the dimples.

"And I'm Sapphire," stated the blue eyed, blonde girl, donning the white flower.

"We're from Australia. Gold Coast," added her friend with raven locks. Eager, I approached them and sat down, with many questions on my mind.

"Nice to meet you. I'm Canadian. It's my first day and they made me change," I stated, attempting to exonerate myself from blame in my fashion mishap. Diamond eyed me, seeming to understand, and said in her adorable Aussie accent.

"No worries. It's happened to the best of us. It's just their disgusting control tactics. You can wear what you want, except pants, when you come in on a *dohan*. If you get a good custie that *dohans* you, you can do whatever you want and wear whatever you want."

"What's a custie and what's a *dohan*?" I asked, having heard the word so many times already.

"Aww. You're so cute, so innocent," Diamond sighed. "Keep that. The custies will love it. A 'custie' is a customer and a *dohan* is when you go out to dinner with the customer and bring him to the club at nine," she explained.

"I never use the word *dohan* in front of a custie because I don't think they like to be reminded that they are paying for your time. Besides if Sato likes you, you've got it made," Sapphire remarked. I did not have time to wonder who Sato was because I was a bit overwhelmed by the *dohan* issue.

"We all have our stories. We're here saving money for plastic surgery. We simply can't go another month with these tiny tits, and we know a fabulous surgeon in Brazil," Diamond giggled, as she gestured to her own perfect set with misplaced, perceptible revulsion.

"We also want to save money and spend a couple months in Thailand together," Sapphire added, though she did not seem as convinced as Diamond about going under the knife.

"So why are *you* here?" Diamond asked. Though it was awkward sharing such personal information, I opened up.

"I'm a songwriter/singer and I need money to manufacture my CD and promote my music," I confided.

"That's cool as!" Diamond responded.

"Do you like *karaoke*?" chimed Sapphire, smiling.

"I've never tried it, but tonight will be an experience. When I get a microphone in my hand, I'm like a different woman." The girls nodded, encouraging me.

It was true. One of my earliest childhood memories was admiring my mother's lone silhouette in the door to my room. The guitar was held in her expert hands and it sweetly lulled us to sleep each night. The songs were mostly about social issues and growing up as a Canadian First Nations woman in a time when racism was widely accepted. One of her songs went something like,

> *Well c'mon all of you fascist pukes*
> *When I see your face I say yes to nukes*
> *We are a moral sorority*
> *Gettin rid of you is priority!*

And so on. We have remained her biggest fans, though she still performed regularly and had sold many CDs.

Like so many other women who began work as a hostess, I started out with a lie. I had not told my mother what I was about to do because I did not want to worry her. She was convinced I would be working as a bartender in Japan.

Until then, I could tell my mother anything and I took pride in our closeness. But for the first time, I decided to keep a secret. I was not yet ready to share it, even with my own mother. I couldn't think about her though, as it would bring nostalgic tears to my eyes. I needed to focus.

Right before nine o'clock, about ten more women flew through the doors, their movements almost seeming synchronized. They had gone through the same awkward procedures that I did before joining the Dog Box crew.

They had accomplished the impossible by changing their clothes in such a small space, surrounded by other women, as close as sardines. I was sure the ten girls bending down to put on their high heels were getting a face full of some other girl's ass. It was an unpleasant thought I never imagined entertaining.

Before I had a chance to even ask for names, the energy of the club changed. A buzz spread throughout the room and all I caught was a single whispered word, "Elvis!" Girls discreetly checked their reflections in small compact mirrors, stuck their chests out and sat up a little bit straighter, with painted plastic smiles. I followed suit.

Huge Hair was joined by a fidgety Mikey at the entrance to the club. As the elevator doors opened, I found myself on the edge of my seat, craning my neck to see who would enter and who deserved that amount of fuss. I wondered if it was a celebrity. The doors opened and a tall, rakish figure, clad in a sleek ivory suit, swept into the room with an air of prestige. His shirt was half open, exposing his bare chest. He looked like the king of the castle.

He came over to the Dog Box and burst into song, "*Wise men say... Only fool rush in...*" He serenaded in an opera-like baritone. "I want all girls at my table and get them some champagne. The best you have!" he demanded, eying us.

"Is Dom...?" Mikey recommended as he showed a weathered menu. He was drooling over the expected profit this customer would produce.

"Yes. Yes." The impatient customer waived him and the menu away. "And two plates of fruit!" the big spender added. Judging from the happy grins the girls exchanged, I gathered fruit was loved by all.

Mikey sprinted off. Everyone stood up and waited around awkwardly. I would have to follow their lead. I wasn't getting any kind of training. It seemed Mikey was seating us according to some vague plan. I was seated first. Mikey presented me to an antsy man, "Rose from Canada. She's new," he announced. They both watched me with expectant smiles.

I extended my hand, which he grasped in a forceful grip. "Hi," I mumbled as I eased onto the couch next to him. The wit and conversation I had considered and rehearsed for my first encounter escaped me.

"Hi. I'm Hiro," he said, sizing me up.

Diamond and Sapphire greeted him with an energetic, "Hiro-Elvis!" and gave him a kiss on opposite cheeks in unison. I wondered why the seat across from him was empty. Perhaps he was expecting a colleague?

Just then, I heard a tinkling laugh that reminded me of a wind chime, and I looked up in expectation, trying to pinpoint the source. "No Mikey. That just won't do," the voice continued. "That's bullocks. I need mangoes (she pronounced it *mahhngoes*, ever so classy) with that fruit platter. You know they're my favorite," she gently scolded.

Potential catastrophe averted, she turned her expert gaze on the table, sauntered across the room and plopped down next to Hiro-Elvis. Patting his knee, she proceeded to start the party. "Hello Darlings," she began, smile dazzling. "Who's ready to hear Hiro serenade us with his angelic voice?"

All the girls started cheering, as if their lives depended on who whooped loudest. When three bottles of Dom Perignon Rosé arrived we eagerly raised our glasses in unified cheers. I was careful to keep my glass lower than everyone else as a sign of respect, remembering the only advice that Barbie gave me. Things got even better when he whipped out his fat wallet and gave every girl at the table an *ichiman* tip. We were even more compliant and flattering as we imagined how we would spend our tip. I would be buying groceries.

The three bottles were finished off quickly, only to be replaced by three more. Before I knew it, I had lost track of the number of glasses of champagne I had consumed. I wasn't used to drinking, so I tried to pace myself. As I watched the blush-colored champagne cascade into my glass, I felt an irresistible urge to get drunk and enjoy the hell out of my first night in Tokyo.

Considering the only other times I drank champagne, I realized my experience was lacking, consisting of a mere glass or two at ordinary, unmemorable weddings. I deserved a night of simple debauchery and indulgence. I would start out that indulging by singing a *karaoke* song. It was the precise moment that my addiction began.

Karaoke addiction, that is. The strongest person could not resist its lure. Hiro-Elvis was the epitome of the addict. Excited, he searched through the small, square digital *karaoke* machine for songs. Later, I found out that he was a regular at the club.

When I attempted *karaoke*, I found it a lot harder than I had thought. For all my bragging about being a musician, I stunk at *karaoke* that first time. Someone had already requested Mariah Carey when I found out her impossibly high, four key range, lyrical interpretations did not suit my decidedly alto voice. *My apologies to Mariah!*

Diamond and Sapphire seemed disappointed and I expected Hiro to be as well, but he smiled at me and rubbed my shoulder, sympathetic. The champagne was working its magic and my inhibitions were dropping fast. I leaned over to talk to Hiro, but I got distracted by the girl with the wind chime laugh. I introduced myself and asked her name.

"Tiffany," she stated abruptly, giving me a look that meant, *Don't you dare lean across my customer like that!* Then she resumed staring at Hiro, as if in love. *How boring*, I thought as I refilled my champagne glass for the umpteenth time. I glanced over and saw Mikey eyeing me, as if trying to send me a telepathic message. I did not have to be a mind reader to know he wanted me to engage the customer.

"So, what are your hobbies, Hiro?" I was grasping for a conversation topic. He looked over with eyes I could not penetrate.

"What are you doing tomorrow night?" he asked.

"I don't know. I don't have any plans," I answered. "I just arrived in Tokyo a few hours ago."

"Tell Mikey to get you to meet me at Almondo's at six thirty tomorrow night," he insisted. He pulled out a pair of huge, gold aviator sunglasses and a red velvet pouch, containing a pair of fake sideburns. He stood and attached the fake hair to his face. "I need Elvis!" he belted. "*All Shook Up* – three keys down!"

As he readied himself for some sort of crazy performance, he gave me one last look. At that point, I knew why he was called Elvis. He was *The King of Roppongi*. After every song he sang, the applause was deafening. Hostesses and staff alike were cheering and whooping. My hands were itchy from clapping overload. And every time we finished clapping, he bowed, discouraging our flattery while ordering his next song.

Hiro stayed for quite a long time, but before I knew it, he paid the exorbitant check and left. I reveled in the time I got to sit in the Dog Box, talking with the girls, but when I looked around the club, I realized it was packed. My hostessing questions would have to wait until later.

Through my tipsy haze, I spotted five cozy tables with people seated. One had a single customer and single hostess in an intimate conversation, while others held Japanese businessmen, dressed in dark suits along with various numbers of animated hostesses. The women's well coifed hair bounced as they laughed, while men told jokes and amused them with fantastic tales.

Mikey showed me to a table with only one man, surrounded by four bubbly women, Sapphire and Diamond included. He made the same introduction as before and gestured with his hand, an indication I was to sit right next to the customer.

The first thing that struck me about my second customer was his appearance. He was particularly unattractive, with pale, almost translucent yellow skin and huge, dark patches around his close-set eyes. He was ghoulish. I noticed his air of grandeur next. He was similar to Hiro-Elvis in that way, dressed impeccably and smelling great. His presence demanded the energy of everyone around him, and in that environment, people were eager to give it.

"What a lucky man you are!" Diamond whispered after I sat next to her. "Five women to look after your every need, you cutie!" She pinched his cheek.

"Your song!" Sapphire yelled as I watched all the girls drag him onto the dance floor, swaying around him, like he was the star of his own music video. The song was *I Love You, Baby* by Paul Anka, but they had substituted his name, Shishi, for "Baby." They were screaming, *I Love You, Shishi, and if it's quite all right...* The scene was hilarious. He looked happy as he began to dance. He started busting it. He did the *moonwalk* and the *cha cha*, and he even grabbed one of the girls and did a crazy, drunken *mambo*, twirling the girl around the room until everyone collapsed at the table, panting, as the song ended.

I was feeling the alcohol as I glanced around the room. Normally, such crazy behavior would attract attention in a small club, but no one seemed to notice our shenanigans. Most of the other tables were rambunctious as well.

There was a random dude in the middle of the floor, engaging himself in what appeared to be "the dance of a randy chicken on speed." He wore his tie around his head, Rambo style, as he twisted and kicked wildly. He was unaware of the clapping hostesses around him, trying to keep him from falling over. His colleagues egged him on, gleeful that he would be the next day's water cooler victim. It was such a contrast to what I expected.

The most sedate table by far was Natasha's. Her solo customer began his song as she looked on. It was a downright adoring stare that didn't falter in consistency. The object of her attention looked dazed as he belted out a Beatles song, pretending not to notice her staring. Their table was anticlimactic in comparison to ours.

Mikey brought a bottle of Sambuca to our table. Diamond cackled and poured a shot directly into Sapphire's waiting mouth. Then she grabbed her lighter and lit her friend's open mouth on fire! I was flabbergasted. But amazingly, Sapphire's expression was one of joy as she closed her mouth and swallowed.

"Rose! You should try Diamond's Flaming Sambuca!" they encouraged, as I tried to wipe the terrified look off my face. I was beginning to recognize there were two types of hostesses, and they were polar opposites. It was because each custie needed to receive artificial worship in one of two different ways: an insane, fun, party way, or in a private, intimate and conservative manner. They were both interesting to me, but at that moment, I wanted to party.

When Shishi got up to use the restroom, the shotgun discussions started up around the table. "Let's just keep him dancing and he'll be happy." Diamond knew him well and loved it when he came in.

"He usually stays all night. I think Rose should be on singing duty," Sapphire decided.

"Right, Sapphire," Diamond whispered. "Can you please desist from conversation in regard to the issue that his socks don't match his suit? His socks are great. His hair's great. His skin's great. He's fucking great."

"Okay, but you are on dance duty," Sapphire insisted. "Diamond is the best dancer in the club, Rose. No, she's the best dancer in Roppongi."

"Done," Diamond smiled. Just then, Shishi came back from the fastest piss known to mankind. He was anxious to resume the party.

"Rose, can you sing *Billy Jean* by Michael Jackson?" Sapphire asked, eying Shishi as he jumped up in delight and continued shaking his booty. When the song began, Diamond got up and they began to shimmy together, while the rest of the exhausted hostesses watched in admiration, clapping. And she *was* a great dancer!

We were working as a team. Throughout the night, I sat at about ten different tables in various states of party mode. I sat with a man they called The Crow, checking him for signs of bird characteristics. A long, beaky nose, shiny raven hair and beady eyes would have sufficed. But all I saw was a short man with a broad face, broken teeth, squinting eyes and long whiskers that sprouted from his sunken chin.

To my surprise as soon I started talking to him, I forgot all about his physical appearance and really enjoyed him as a person. I was ashamed to think that I would never have talked to The Crow in Canada. If we met in a club, I would probably not have given him the time of day, and it saddened me to realize just how shallow I was.

But there we were in Tokyo, having a great time together. I found out that he lived for rock and roll *karaoke* music. He squeaked out his chosen songs in a rollicking mumble, one after the other. I was all too happy to keep recommending his songs, though Mikey and Huge Hair seemed to be in agony through their fake smiles and clapping hands.

It turned out The Crow was the father of twins, who always dreamed of going to America to pursue a career as a rock star. As he shared, he looked so shy and innocent that I felt a sort of protectiveness and a need to help him.

As we sat there, Mikey came to the table and motioned with a universal phone mime that I had a call. *Who the hell was calling me?* The only person I had told the truth to about where I was going was my twin and Barbie, but neither of them had the phone number to the club.

It turned out I didn't have a phone call at all. It was a ruse to get me into the office, so they could tell me to get the clients' name cards. I would need to call them tomorrow, thank them and possibly get a *dohan*. I thought that move was pushy, but I guessed I couldn't be an introvert in the hostess world.

I was returned to The Crow, where I easily got his name card and a promise of dinner. It was ridiculous how happy I was, to be going out to dinner with a man that I would never look at twice in Canada. That sense of satisfaction was weird, but it did not carry over to every customer because some of them should be in mental hospitals.

During the night, I sat with a dirty doctor. That guy just wanted to have his belly rubbed all night. He wore foundation and a wig, and his clinical aftershave stung my nose. After an exhausting hour of trying to think up interesting questions, I excused myself to the ladies room to smoke my hidden doobie. I returned renewed, armed with an air of skunk, perfume and creative new conversation topics.

Another memorable custie was the man who would only introduce himself as Prince. He repeatedly sang the same song, while crossing himself, Catholic style, over and over. I tried to laugh at first, and then I just ignored him and was removed from the table.

I found that most girls did not mind sitting with the crazies. As long as they were requested, they would sit with just about any customer. They found it amusing to compare crazy stories, while also feeling sorry for them. One thought nagged me as I scanned the room: so far I had not seen one hot customer.

Just as I was beginning to consider the possibility that all the customers would be unattractive, a vision of masculinity breezed in the door. Maybe it was just the fact that he was so hot in comparison to other custies. Maybe I wouldn't have thought he was fine in "real life." Maybe I was drunk and horny. *Who knew?* But I was drooling.

The pristine white suit he wore clung to his body and his presence was noticed by every sly female eye in the room. His exotic eyes were disguised beneath grey tinted, platinum sunglasses. I could not help but notice his structured jaw, perfect nose and sensual, full lips. He was an excellent specimen of a man.

I eyed up Mikey with a huge smile, in an attempt to show that I was all too available to be persuaded to sit with that sex god. He could twist my rubber arm and I wouldn't complain. That didn't work, as neither Mikey nor the hottie paid any attention to me.

That was when I realized that he was not alone. The yummy man stood beside a pale, bent, Japanese man in his mid-fifties, with round, tinted, gold framed glasses. The older man smiled, at no one in particular, but the warmth didn't reach his eyes.

The pair were ushered to a secluded corner and joined by Natasha, Anna and Svetlana. Natasha sat down next to the older man and Anna sat by the younger, hunky guy and tossed her blonde curls, acting coquettish.

That's when people started brownnosing up a shitstorm. They were dashing about with star struck eyes, as if those dudes were descending from Olympus. One waiter flew over and began mixing drinks, and Mikey grinned, looking like a weasel, baring his neglected teeth and hovering.

That man clearly was some sort of boss. Yet, he looked so normal. I wouldn't pick him out of a crowd to be unusual. Everyone was speaking what sounded like fluent Japanese. I envied that. It was frustrating being unable to express myself. But I guess that feeling was part of my new identity and I was going to try to enjoy that change.

The subservient, reverent attitudes directed toward that power table indicated he was a man of impressive power. I wanted to surround myself with it.

I wanted to sit at that table because the younger man interested me. Lust invaded my heart. I *wanted* him! Just then, something great and terrible happened. He looked at me.

He deliberately focused his attention on me, staring straight into my eyes with a dark, intense look. His eyes began to travel down my body and the heat of his gaze was that of a touch. The man had game.

But then with one last glance, I saw that his eyes were cold, black glass. The warmth I thought that I saw must have emanated from my own imagination. I tried unsuccessfully to concentrate on the custie in front of me. He was just plain dull, but I was already getting really good at multitasking.

I could just sit at the table with the right smile and nod, occasionally adding a "ya?" or "really?" to the conversation. All the while, I was planning out my life, like what to do tomorrow, or missing my twin, or imagining in intricate detail a wild sexcapade with a certain Japanese man who was too nearby for comfort.

If I were the handsome man, I wouldn't have been caught dead in that seedy club. Yet instead of his presence in the hostess club disgusting me, it captivated me. I still couldn't get over the fact that men paid money for that kind of casual company. Being the inquisitive, stubborn person I was I couldn't wait to get to the bottom of it.

At that point on my first night, the alcohol began to take a more noticeable effect. Things started getting hazy. I regretted the two shots of tequila with my last custie, Tequila-Masa. The last thing I remembered was cramming into an elevator, reeking of booze, with a crazy crew of people.

Red-faced, bright-eyed salary men, hardcore hostesses and custie/hostess teams sang and partied the lift all the way to the bottom. At every floor, the door would open, revealing a completely different scene. Some were luxurious, plush, clubs in which only beautifully bejeweled, Japanese girls were employed. They all had teased hair and high pitched, nasal voices.

Another floor exposed a smoky, dark club, with girls in lingerie hustling about, singing *karaoke*. An annoying beep signaled that the elevator had exceeded its weight limit, so the jostling assemblage got shoved back into Mikey's. They were a drunken, motley bevy, desperately hanging on to the bitter end.

Finally downstairs, I tried to follow them, wondering what Roppongi had in store for the rest of the evening. Unfortunately, my plans were thwarted when Mikey appeared out of nowhere to usher me into a cab, waiting to take me home for my curfew check.

THE MORNING (AFTERNOON)
AFTER THE FIRST DAY OF THE REST OF MY LIFE

The inky eyes gazing into mine held unmentionable sorrow. They had a depth that captivated me. He leaned over ever so slowly, until he was a breath away. I had been waiting for it. I smiled and waited for the kiss that would change my life.

Something was wrong, however. As I glanced down, I realized we were standing embraced on the ledge of a steep, foreboding tower. He agonized, staring into my eyes, and then he just... pushed me off the edge. I fell, lost in the misty void below.

I woke with a flailing start, having no idea where I was. It was a weird feeling, as I lied on a narrow bunk bed, several feet off the ground, with tears running from my burning eyes. On my right was a pile of dirty clothes, reeking of cigarette smoke, while to my left was a half eaten McDonald's cheeseburger, mashed into the threadbare blue and white checkered sheets.

Locating my contact case next to the pillow, I peeled the grainy lenses out of my eyes and sighed with relief. Snoring from the bottom bunk revealed a peek at bare legs and blonde hair. It could have been anyone. I tried to forget my disturbing dream as I slid from the bunk and rummaged through my purse for my cell phone to check the time: 4:20. Nice! First things first, tokage! I rolled up a fatty, slipped out on the miniature balcony covered in various junky objects, and made short work of my doobie.

Just then, I heard the sound of girls having fun in the other room, and the spectacular smell of bacon and eggs reached my nose. I slipped into the kitchen and surveyed the scene. Diamond was busy cooking up a feast at the tiny stove. She was adept at utilizing the small space, as she piled dishes of food in every available corner, even on the floor.

Sapphire was meticulously setting a small table with mismatched, chipped crockery and four sets of disposable chopsticks. She grinned at me and exclaimed, "You must be hungry. Let's have some brekkie, it's the only thing that will wake Tiffany before five p.m."

"Is that who I share a room with?" I was a tad nervous about it, as Tiffany and I did not hit it off well the night before.

"There's Di and me in one room. Natasha, Anna and Svetlana are in another room. They are all at Japanese school right now. You and Tiffany are in the last room," Sapphire answered as she padded around in white, fluffy rabbit slippers. *Holy shit! Seven girls in one apartment!* All of a sudden, a phone rang with the tune *I'm a Hustla, Baby* by Jay Z, and Tiffany appeared in all her naked glory.

"Oy! Can't you lot keep it down out there? A young lady needs her beauty sleep," she teased.

"I knew the bacon would get you up," giggled Diamond, while trying to use the chopsticks. Polish Monica said you had a pair of stockings ripped off your body last night in Sport's."

"I was on the D.B. from hell, but I ended up making an acceptable amount of cash," Tiffany yawned. *What the hell did their conversation mean?* Sapphire recognized my confusion and explained.

"Polish Monica is one of the many Monicas we know," she said. "She works at Sport's, which is a drink back bar, hence the term D.B. If you take a customer to a drink back bar and he orders bottles of champers or wine, you can get a fifty percent kickback from the customer's total bill." She continued, "So, which custie ripped your stockings off and how much was the bill?"

"We had three bottles of Verve Cliquot Rosé," Tiffany answered. "They were around ¥50,000 each, plus about ¥30,000 in entry charges, food and shots. So, fifty percent of ¥180,000 is ¥90,000, which is about six hundred fifty pounds." She was good at math. "I'll give you one guess who the custie is," she teased.

"TG!" Diamond and Sapphire answered in unison.

"Tokyo Gigolo is possibly the most loathsome, yet economically beneficial custie I've ever known," Tiffany laughed. "There was a run in my tights, and you know how obsessive compulsive he is. The moment I wasn't looking, he ripped them off me in the blink of an eye. He is so dodgy. Monica was absolutely pissing herself!"

What worried me most about traveling to Japan? Men! Men seemed a species of their own, while I had limited experience with them. I had a long-term boyfriend until right before I left, but because I had not dated anyone else in so long, I was self-conscious and sensitive about being out there. Hostessing required personal charm, confidence and a thick skin. The latter would be one of the biggest challenges of the industry for me.

"By the way, who covered for me last night at curfew phone call?" Tiffany inquired.

"I did," Diamond nodded, and she began to imitate Tiffany's posh accent. "Mikey, it's Tiffany. I'm knackered. This is *intolerable*! Good evening."

"Innumerable thanks, Darling!" Tiffany laughed, again with the elongated "a" sound. I loved it. It was catchy. *Dahhhling!*

"So, how was your first night, Rose?" Sapphire asked as Diamond placed a huge lumberjack breakfast in front of me. *How was my first night?* I was still overwhelmed, but that sense was accompanied by an excitement about what would happen next.

"It was awesome and crazy. Unforgettable!" I acknowledged. "Thank you! This food looks amazing."

An annoying, loud cell phone rang, causing us all to jump. It turned out to be someone calling for me. The girl who had the phone before me must have been deaf to the offensive ring tone. It had to be the club "Hello?" I asked a bit annoyed, because I wanted to finish my food.

"Hi. This is Takeshi," a halting voice answered. It was Huge Hair. "You have *dohan* tonight 6:30 with Hiro-Elvis. I coming to your apartment 6:00, to walk you Roppongi."

"Okay. See you soon," I replied. Great! That left me an hour to get ready, and I had to do a complete overhaul – the works, including leg shaving and nails! *Well, I better get cracking*, I thought. When I re-entered the kitchen, all the girls were at the table, with stacks of name cards, talking about custies.

"Are you going to ring the dirty doctor? He's like in love with you this week," Diamond joked to Sapphire, with a twinkle in her mischievous eyes.

"Ugh! That's my last resort," Sapphire groaned. "I'm going to try Taka-Depp first. He`s usually good for a *dohan*. What about you, Tiffany? Are you going to dinner with your boyfriend, TG?"

"It is so embarrassing being seen in public with him," Tiffany sighed. "I think that he actually tries to make himself appear less attractive. I thought I might call Hiro-Elvis." Undisclosed to me, I was part of an unwanted love triangle.

"Guys, I have a *dohan* with Hiro-Elvis tonight," I admitted. "I'm sorry Tiffany. Maybe you can come, too?" I did not want to start any drama.

Diamond laughed and said, "Look. You've had a good run with him, Tiff. He is so unpredictable. He's an absolute womanizer and every hostess knows it."

Tiffany looked put-off for all of two seconds, and then she shrugged, "Right. It was brilliant for the week it lasted, but *c'est la vie*." She put a confiding arm around my shoulder and remarked, "Milk it for all its worth while you can, Rose." With that she turned in one fluid, graceful movement to pick up her cell phone and made herself the object of some other customer's obsessive night. "Masa! I miss you and I am absolutely famished!" she emoted as she stepped onto the veranda.

I still needed clarification about one issue. I could not forget the pleasure or the horror of my recent dreams. The man who pushed me off the tower was, of course, the icy eyed, handsome man from the night before.

"One question, Sapphire," I asked. "Who was that at the last table in the far corner with the hottie? What's up with that?"

"Oh!" laughed Sapphire, "Don't you think he's adorable? That's Ryu. The suave, older guy is Sato. He's the owner of the club. Ryu is kind of like his assistant. Basically, if Sato likes you, you have it made. He is currently besotted with Natasha, but he is easily swayed," she said.

"Hey Diamond! Your stalker is calling," Sapphire announced. Diamond rushed forward, serious. She turned the Cypress Hill song down and made a face at Sapphire while seeking privacy. She settled on her only option – the top bunk. She frowned and shut the paper thin door in our grinning faces.

"Hi baby. What's new?" I heard her say.

"Di has a stalker, otherwise known as her boyfriend," Sapphire said. "This man makes the CIA look like amateurs. He calls her like clockwork at specific times of the day, and if she doesn't answer, it isn't a problem for him, because he has a GPS location for her on his phone and can track her down anywhere. It's insane. The weird thing is that he actually knows the truth about her job. He encourages her to make as much money as possible, but he is still watching every step she makes. She likes strange men," she giggled. Sapphire thought it was hilarious, while I thought it was kind of scary.

"What about you, Sapphire? Do you have an old ball and chain?" I asked.

"I just got out of a four year relationship and I am enjoying my independence," she confided. "I'm dating several lucky, young men at the moment, I'll have you know. One is the physical double of Brad Pitt – bleach blonde hair and a cocky swagger. Yet he's shit in bed. Who does he think he is?"

"And who else?" I wondered aloud.

"I'm also dating a gorgeous Japanese man, who speaks no English. He is so shy and quiet. He never talks. I never used to be into Japanese guys, probably because I have never been around Japanese people before. But the longer you're here, the hotter they get. And the small dick thing is a farce. This boy has it going on. He's a freak between the sheets."

"Some of your slang sounds American. Have there been American girls here?" I asked.

"Yeah, some of our lingo gets completely mixed up with so many international women in the house. But two American girls just finished their contracts. One broke the other's arm!" Sapphire added.

"What?" I was aghast.

Sapphire noted my stunned face and continued, "No, it wasn't like that. We were having an arm wrestling competition in the club. We have contests sometimes, like rock-scissors-paper or *karaoke*. People get bored and they want to change things up. Thankfully, I lost out in the first round. When the prize is an *ichiman* or a broken arm, I'm going to go with a working limb."

"I do not understand something here," I interrupted.

"I'll explain," she insisted. "The final contestants were the two American girls. One was a professional softball pitcher and the other girl was a professional bodybuilder. They were both at least one hundred ninety centimeters, around six feet tall. The pitcher literally broke the other girl's arm, snapped the bone in half. The ambulance had to come. The girls both finished their contracts, though. The injured girl finished, wearing evening dresses, while accessorizing them with a flattering cast. But many custies liked the idea of helping a girl in need, so she ended her contract as the number one girl."

"What's the number one girl?" I asked, intrigued.

"Next time you glance around the change room, stage named The Dungeon, just observe the sign listing all of our names and the total amount that our A-Request patrons spend in the club. My name is near the bottom, stemming from the fact that I don't give a shit, and yours is at the bottom because you're new. Natasha is at the top because she has Sato and a few more juicy custies. Tiffany makes the most money, though. That woman is a professional, she's the D.B. queen. She's number two on the list," she added.

"We call drink backs D.B.s. You take your customer to select bars and you get fifty percent back from their bill." Sapphire explained. Just then Tiffany re-entered the room and offered her opinion about the fact that the club rated us.

"That list is bullocks!" she complained. "The only reason I give a shit is because of the bonus. If my clients spend ¥1,000,000 (ten thousand dollars) total in one month, I get an extra ¥150,000 (fifteen hundred dollars). Brilliant! That goes a long way to my credit card debt. At first I wanted to pay off my outrageous student loan, but fuck that! Plus, Justin and I want to go on a holiday somewhere after my visa is up, that stinker!"

"Justin is her boyfriend in England," Sapphire explained.

"Man, it must be hard to be away from him and work in this industry," I commented.

"Of course, he has no idea what I'm *really* involved with out here," Tiffany added. "But he needn't know things that would only hurt him. He thinks that I'm modeling. Anyhow, I'm having a laugh and I'm making money for us. What he doesn't know won't hurt him. Besides, we're soul mates."

That reminded me. I wanted to look beautiful for the evening and that required time, patience and a fabulous wardrobe. "I'll see you in a bit. I need to become divine," I yelled to Sapphire as I chose a sexy, black strapless dress that I could wear at the club, as well as at dinner. Ha ha! I could wear whatever the fuck I wanted that night because I was on a *dohan*. No need to change with the droves in The Dungeon!

That outfit showed just the right amount of tits and legs to be appropriate for both venues. After I straightened my long, blonde hair and painted my nails a glossy black, I decided on a white, cashmere shrug, my new white, wraparound stilettos and a matching purse. Huge gold, dangling earrings completed my fashion statement. I knew Hiro-Elvis wouldn't be able to resist me in that get-up.

Takeshi arrived as pandemonium set in at AZABU TOWERS apartment, #501. I still couldn't get over limited space in Tokyo apartments, but we all managed, dodging each other with practiced, unmistakable precision. The Russian girls had returned from their Japanese lesson and were waiting to get in the shower.

Other hostess needs were in high demand as well, such as nail polish, microwave cheese and white bread sandwiches. The room was decorated with thong underwear which, like small, colorful flowers, we dried on plastic racks. Every few minutes, a frenzied voice would cry out, "Time Check?" Someone, whoever was closest, would look at the clock and exclaim, "it's 5:58 and all is *not* well! Where the hell is my mascara?"

Thank God for Tiffany's photographic memory. "I think I saw a blue tube next to Natasha's knickers by the table!" she yelled from her bottom bunk, which was doubling as her boudoir.

The waiter smiled as he entered the room. It was the first time I saw him smile. He ducked and dodged hanging panties as he surveyed the half naked women surrounding him. He was definitely enjoying himself.

"Go?" he motioned, asking if I was ready.

I shrugged, impressed by his nonchalance and followed him into the cramped elevator and out onto the humid streets of Azabu Juban, Tokyo. Takeshi was a fine man. He was quite a bit taller than me, even in heels, and his broad shoulders and dimples played to my many weaknesses for what I thought were attractive in a man. I hadn't noticed it the night before because of my fury, but he was handsome. "Where are you from, Takeshi?" I asked.

"Japan," he answered with a puzzled look.

"Ya. I kinda guessed that," I nodded, awkward, as I tried to get him to open up. "But where are you from in Japan? And why do you speak such good English?"

"I am from Kyushu." The conversation seemed over. I am a fast walker, but he was starting to open a distance ahead of me. I had to almost gallop to keep up. I wanted to try to continue with my famous ass shaking, model walk, but he was making it difficult. He didn't answer my question about why he spoke such good English and he was beginning to look far less gorgeous with each lengthy stride.

"Hey Takeshi," I called out. "I know my way from here. It's the pink and white sign on the corner. I can meet Elvis by myself." I was through trying to keep up. He shrugged and continued walking, without a word or glance in my direction. Thanks for any help that you *didn't* give me, asshole!

Hopefully not all the fine men in Japan were so rude. Jesus! If I was his girlfriend, I would have kept on walking... in the opposite direction or I would have hailed a cab to get away from him more quickly. Regardless of having his help or not, in Roppongi I got a sense of belonging that I had not known before.

GROWING THE BALLS...

Sometimes, when I was in a horrendous situation, I believed for a few seconds it was nothing more than a bad dream. It was calming, in a weird sense.

"So, what are your views about hostessing and the hostess industry?" Hiro-Elvis asked as he grilled me. I was exhausted.

"Well, seeing as how this is my second day, I can't really give you a clear answer, Hiro. It seems okay, so far. What are *your* views?" I asked. The eager eyes surveying my face were starting to make me ill, causing the scrumptious, two hundred dollar Kobe steak to pitch in my stomach. He was becoming more aggravating with each sentence, and we still had to go to the club.

We had been to a superb restaurant where I was spoiled like a princess. I had to admit the list of pros from the evening was impressive: Hiro showed up at Almondo's with two dozen blood red roses, the restaurant was the best I had ever been to, and the pride I felt at being on a *dohan* so quickly was just the ice cream on the pie. And yet I experienced a sense of loathing.

The major con was that I felt like a piece of meat on display in a butcher shop. Hiro-Elvis said he ate there at least once a week and the staff honored him as a regular. It was the same at Mikey's. People treated him with a reverence usually reserved for someone royal.

The conversation between us consisted of him bragging about how *extremely* wealthy he was. He owned property all over the world, he'd been married four different times to Russian models, and he had trouble deciding which car to drive, Bentley or Lamborghini. His boasting did not impress me. I was bored. I thought I escaped the monotony of serving tables to see all that the world had to offer. I was disappointed.

Kobe was a city, south of Kyoto that specialized in raising the world's finest beef. They massaged and coddled the animals, fed them beer and even in some accounts, allowed them to live in their own homes before slaughtering them.

Hiro-Elvis had the cold eyes of a predatory butcher and I had the wary eyes of a pampered bovine. He was droning on about how dangerous Roppongi was. I tuned him out, buttoning up my pullover a little, against the sudden chill. *Was it the air conditioner or the company?*

I next discovered his second favorite topic: anything morbid. Thus began an abhorrent bombardment of stories, pertaining to anything from bestiality to fatal attacks by monkeys on innocent pedestrians in Northern Japan. It was scary to encounter that part of his mind. No amount of pay was worth that kind of frightful counseling work.

"Don't go to the discos in Roppongi. Crazy people look for girls like you," Hiro warned. "You know the story about Lucie Blackman, *ne*?" he asked with perverse interest. Gleeful, he seemed to be anticipating my terrorized reaction.

Lucie Blackman. It was the case of a British hostess, who was found dead and dismembered in an isolated cave. I was shocked he mentioned it. A slow tremor of terror slid down my spine. I started pinching myself under the table, hard. I was trying to distract myself with pain so I would not lose it.

When the meal was over, Hiro studied me for a long time. As we sat there, Hiro handed me a long, rectangular, navy-blue box. A girl does not expect to be handed a diamond Gucci watch on a first date. But I deserved it after surviving that dinner.

My mom used to tell me a story about how the Canadian aboriginal people believed that if you unloaded your woes on others, you had to supply them with tobacco or blankets or something else of value. The Gucci watch was in essence my blanket. Let's hope it did not have smallpox!

As we strolled along the street together, Hiro was silent and the night air cleared my mind. The diamond glint from the new bauble at my wrist soothed my nerves. On a Roppongi street, a custie was like a prize. Everyone looked at me with envy. A custie as famous as Elvis definitely earned me a few admiring stares, especially from the large, leering touts. I would be embarrassed anywhere else in the world if I was walking down the street with a man old enough to be my father.

After we got to the club, Hiro couldn't help but make a dramatic entrance. As I dressed in The Dungeon, I decided, because of the *dohan*, to take advantage of being able to wear what I wanted. The forbidden, fabulous black number that I wasn't allowed to wear on my first night hugged my curves in all the right places. Instead of opting for the more formal black, strapless dress, I decided to live dangerously. I would try to sneak by with no stockings.

I sauntered out, employing my favorite model walk, oozing self-confidence. Hiro was unimpressed. I expected compliments and eye-popping, but no. I was greeted with a cold stare as I crossed the room and plopped down next to the party in progress.

Unlike the always professional Tiffany, I just didn't seem to be able to muster the energy to keep feeding his ego. Thankfully, Tiffany flanked his other side. He appeared dazed under the brilliance of her flashy smile.

For what seemed the millionth time, I tuned it all out and went about exploring my own mind. Being surrounded by the Japanese language and culture made introspection quite easy. Tiffany seemed fluent in Japanese, while I was basically mute. In some ways I liked it, though. In Canada, people's shit talking could destroy an otherwise clear mind.

I was relieved ten minutes later, when Mikey came to the table and escorted me over to the darkest corner of the club, where a brooding, young Japanese man with sensual lips sat waiting. He reminded me of a Japanese Johnny Depp behind his thick framed glasses and loud, floral print shirt.

"A-Request. First request. You will get three thousand yen next Wednesday. Get phone number. Good customer." Mikey seemed so serious. As I sat down, my strength returned because that man was by far the hottest custie I had ever sat with. I prepared to flirt and turn on my charm, beaming at him with a come-hither air.

That was when I grew balls. I had always been shy with guys before, but I had newfound courage. I extended my hand and introduced myself, trying to make eye contact. He took my hand and mumbled his name, which turned out to be Hiro. I guessed his was a very common name in Japan. But from that moment on, he would always be Hiro-Depp in my mind.

I think everyone is shy in one way or another, but Japanese people seemed to be more introverted. Either Hiro-Depp was extremely shy, or he was a ghost. Sometimes it was like he did not... exist. He didn't even look at me as he gestured for the waiter to get me a drink.

I ordered a glass of white wine and a tepid glass of wine arrived. I asked for a glass of ice, to make it somewhat drinkable. The hostess drink menu was pathetic. The choice was cold tea, wine, or soft drinks, unless the customer was willing to buy a nice bottle.

"*Kampai!*" I tried, but again to no avail. He merely touched his glass to mine and put it back down on the table without drinking or speaking. His pouty lips were turned down into a frown, as he avoided me and cringed away on the edge of his seat. *What the hell was up?* I wondered.

I am a weirdo, which is why I had a real urge to get to the bottom of that mystery man. I wondered why he requested me, if he wanted to ignore me. I knew I was in trouble at that point. My stubborn attitude and my unquenchable thirst for a challenge sometimes created difficult situations.

I abandoned all the usual questions that were standard in every club. I knew, instinctively, that he didn't want to discuss topics like, "Do you live in Tokyo?" or "What are your hobbies?" or "Do you like *karaoke*?" I leaned forward, allowing my long, blonde hair to brush his arm, as I whispered in his ear, "What do you love?"

He looked taken aback, but only for a split second, as he looked me straight in the eyes for the first time. He wasn't a ghost at all. He was very alive. "I love you," he deadpanned.

"You don't even *know* me." I was glad he had come out of his shell.

"I know more than you think. I know you're bored, and I know why you're here." His English was good. One minute, the guy was almost standoffish, and the next minute, he was full on.

"Well, why don't you cure my boredom?" I flirted.

"Cure?" He seemed puzzled by the word.

"Why don't you make me *not bored*," I tried again. He ignored my comment, fingering his whiskey and water on the rocks, thinking.

"Oh! Sorry! I guess I should be filling that, hey?" I forgot I was at work for a second.

Apologetic, I reached over to fill his nearly empty glass, but he brushed my hand away and said,

"No. That's okay. I don't want you to do it." As he looked away, the emotional walls came up around him.

"That's fine by me," I said, sitting back. "I can chill. You can make my drink if you want. I need another ice cube." He relaxed and obliged me.

"So, Mr. Psychic, why am I *here*?" I asked, intrigued.

He paused for so long that I thought he wasn't going to answer. Then he took a deep breath and replied, "You need money, and... you have a dream." He was spot on! It was a simple but plain truth.

Just then Mikey, with his predictably bad timing, ran up to our table, rushing me to the elevator to clamor amongst the girls who were giving Hiro-Elvis a flamboyant farewell. I barely had time to give Hiro-Depp my handwritten business card with my cell number on it. I hurried to the front door before the elevator doors closed. I waved to Elvis, who nodded his head.

I weaved toward the Dog Box with a hopeful look. Thank God, it was already one a.m., only two more hours. Just as I was about to sink into an inviting seat, a whirlwind breezed into the club, in the form of a very drunken Shishi.

Mikey waived me over and hissed in my ear, "A-request." Then as an afterthought, "Don't let him fall down." I guess I still had some hostessing to do.

BUTTERSCOTCH PUNANI

Sunlight beamed like lasers through a crack in the curtains, its beam directly searing my sensitive retinas. I did not know where the hell I was. I lifted my head, but the splitting headache and dull throbbing of a hangover made me groan aloud.

An arm from behind gripped me across the chest while strange fingers trailed up my bare thigh, threatening to start a morning session. I could only imagine or assume what had happened the night before. *Shit! I was in a love hotel!*

Bits of memories flashed through my mind at irregular intervals, like a movie I had watched, but was not in. The last thing I could remember was Shishi being carried to a taxi, passed out drunk. The girls had continued ordering drinks and food, and were having a blasty-blast with *karaoke*, as Shishi snoozed angelic, oblivious to the raucous party around him.

I was stumbling home when I got the call. 090 7654 6969! It was definitely someone kinky with those digits. "*Moshi Moshi.*" That was my new expression. It was how the Japanese said hello on the phone, and I loved the sound of it. It was cute.

"Let's continue our talking. Meet me at Almondo's. Let's keep drink," a sexy voice intoned.

I had a weakness for husky voices. I was not done for the evening and I was massively randy. *Was I a slut for having slept with him the first night?* Yes, by most people's standards.

But *slut* was just an ugly word used by some people who would rather pass on fantabulous, mind blowing, earth shattering sex. Life is short, tomorrow is not guaranteed. Hiro-Depp turned out to be a freak between the sheets, who praised my pussy in delicious ways, never tiring. He treated it like, in his words, "Butterscotch!"

I have a huge sexual appetite with no qualms about it. I hadn't been laid in months, so I was a deviant who needed to release myself. I could have chosen masturbation, but I have limited space at my apartment, with the bunk beds and all.

I probably would have been fantasizing about something fabulous, like making love in a wheat field to my totally hot high school gym teacher, when BOOM! – some unwanted custie's warped wiener would wander into my fantasy. Who knew what trauma would befall my sexuality at such a thought. No, I needed to take a lover.

I paid my respects to the love hotel. I woke up on a round rotating bed, in a room with mirrors on the ceiling and a pool for skinny dipping. It's a good thing I figured a way around the five o'clock curfew, or that night would have cost me five hundred dollars.

Genius that she was, Sapphire could imitate my Canadian accent to perfection. When Mikey called, she pretended to be me. I was under strict instructions to begin practicing Australian, British and Russian accents so I could reciprocate.

I sprung out of bed and started searching for my panties to prepare for the walk of shame. Hiro was just lying there, completely naked, with a huge grin on his face.

"You go?" he asked.

"Ya, I gotta... um run." The room was closing in on me.

"Call me. You have my number on your phone. Let's do it again," he called as I made my getaway. I stumbled out of the room, wobbling into the sunshine, passing happy, traditional families who avoided looking at me. I wished I had brought sunglasses the night before.

THE OUTSKIRTS

I survived my first week. I could not believe I longed for the Dog Box a few days earlier. I surfed the Dog Box all that next night. I had to sit there and watch people drink, eat and sing. It got old fast. The hostessing industry was like a roller coaster. The moment before an exhilarating plunge into the unknown could last forever. That was the waiting area. You were on the outside, looking in.

I got in trouble for hosting my own Dog Box parties, telling jokes galore, and trying to get to know everyone. I found out the management (a.k.a. "The Man") did not want the customers to know we were having a good time without them. He wanted us to look like we were just hoping to be sat with the custies. When we were not with custies, we were supposed to look bored and pitiful.

That was The Outskirts. I did not plan on hanging out there for long. Its opposite part was the roller coaster, or wave. It was definitely a place I had visited before. I went there on a *dohan* with Shishi earlier that night.

We ate *yakiniku*, which turned out to be a delicious and spicy, garlic rich meal. It was also interactive, with a huge grill in the middle that we kept covering with superb beef strips, prawns and veggies. Using our chopsticks, we smothered them in a special, dark, delicious sauce before stuffing the hulking bites into our waiting mouths. We wore enormous paper bibs like we were giant babies. I loved it!

It was the first time I had sat down one-on-one with Shishi while we were both sober, and he was a breath of fresh air. He regaled me with fascinating stories, one after another. Working as an interpreter, he met all kinds of people. He had cocktails with Cyndi Lauper, who he said was lovely, but had a foul mouth. He had been to the Japanese emperor's palace and met the royal family. He was appalled when I called his stock market fortune "gambling" and tried all night to teach me otherwise.

"Gambling to me implies more luck than skill," he sniffed. Shishi was obviously bi-sexual. He was an equal balance of pent-up male and female sexual energy. I could tell right away. While on a *dohan* with me, he was constantly full of colorful comments like, "Mikey has a big dick!" and "Takeshi sucks massive balls!" It didn't put me off. I just laughed at his outrageous comments.

Still, he liked women enough to keep a few of his favorites around. "That suits me great," he would tell me, trying to make sure I did not get jealous. I enjoyed the hell out of that part of the roller coaster. He was so entertaining in that I never knew what he would do next.

I learned something about myself and my flaws as we walked back to the club together. *Why was it okay to judge people on their looks?* Looks fade over time. They had nothing to do with knowing a person. But I enjoyed being around hot people. Everyone did, and that was natural.

When I was going out with my girls, I ran around coordinating our outfits for a gorgeous team effect. I wanted to be seen as desirable. It was fun. But if I focused on the superficial, I could be missing out on meeting amazing people. I would not let that happen to me.

What if *I* had been born Shishi? The superficial usually judge on looks. Shishi was unattractive. Sad but true, and even more pitiful, most people who met Shishi would never know his true beauty. They would see him as a Phantom of the Opera type figure, a monster, only to be pitied.

He had the misfortune of being born into a consumer-based, sexist society that told him as a young boy his worth was based on numbers. He was a statistic, rather than an individual. The club was his outlet and one of his only ways of rebelling against "The Man."

I had a bright reverent moment where I saw the world clearly for a millisecond, but only a millisecond. The light receded and only allowed me a grateful glimpse. I had the horrible feeling I had forgotten something and I could not quite remember what it was. It was on the tip of my tongue.

For the first time in my life, I was having a recurring nightmare. It was a bizarre dream where Ryu kissed me and then pushed me off the top of a high place. It was haunting me every night. A silvery peal of laughter made me recall the object of my torment.

I glanced over at the darkest table in the farthest corner of the room and saw Natasha at her best. Her svelte frame was draped, preening over Sato-san as he glared down into his hot tea. The tea probably had some sort of mystical medicine in it to soothe his ailments, as he was always grumbling about being tired from diabetes.

I didn't really care about Sato-san. I was trying to avoid the torture of seeing Ryu with Anna. Not able to curb my morbid fascination, I turned and surveyed the scene, jealous. Anna and Ryu were deep in conversation, as Ryu's arm dangled over the back of her seat. Her eyes were glued to his as she spoke with him in Japanese. She flipped her bright red hair over her shoulder and filled his whiskey and water.

Jealousy was poison. It was especially toxic in a place like that. *Why was I wasting my time? What was it about Ryu that drove me so crazy?*

Without warning, everything changed. First, Hiro-Depp walked into the room, slouched shouldered, not looking at anyone. At the same time, Sato-san jumped up from his table and screamed *"Baka!"* at Natasha and stormed out. Ryu followed. Natasha was devastated.

After I sat down with Hiro-Depp as his "A-Request," I decided to take my own advice about compassion and invited Natasha to sit with us. She needed to get her mind off anything club-related. "Let's sing!" I called out, and we proceeded to have a great night!

THE WORKING POOR

Every day at five o'clock, a strange, melancholy song played on loudspeakers all around Japan. To school children, it was a signal to go home for dinner, but for some night workers, it served as an alarm. I had been there for three weeks and I was getting antsy with all the rules at the club. Every day was a struggle. I wanted to tell "The Man" to *fuck off*!

Everyone had something they hated about the club. Most of us dreaded "*skebbae*," which was a perverted, or a "skabby" custie. I had not been sat with a *skebbae* until then, but I knew it was only a matter of time before my luck would run out.

To help new girls cope with skabby customers and to prepare them for the inevitable worst, Mikey and Huge Hair put on a humorous pantomime, as a sort of classroom lesson at a meeting one day. Mikey played the hostess, surprisingly well, and Huge Hair was the groping customer. Huge Hair brought it on: roaming hands, love hotel innuendos and crude jokes.

All that Mikey, "the pro hostess," did to combat the horrid advances was to grasp the roaming hands in his vice grip, smiling. I laughed and told myself I would not put up with that kind of degrading behavior, no matter what anyone paid me. Another humiliating experience we had to endure in the club was getting weighed every week. Our job was to drink and when we drank, we got hungry.

Our food menu consisted of fatty foods like pizza, pasta and fried chicken. In addition, we sat for eight hours a day. It was not an ideal environment to maintain a nice figure. Some girls would do anything to avoid being weighed.

Monday was the dreaded weigh day, and you could bet your ass every girl was turning on the charm and calling every custie she knew to try to get a *dohan* to escape it. It was one of the club's trade tactics and it worked for them. Monday was rarely slow.

It was pointless to weigh us because customers were different and liked different body shapes and personalities in girls. The regulars who came to Mikey's obviously liked Western girls' curves and individuality. Most of my custies thought I was too thin, and they were forever trying to fatten me up. However, I began to realize that not all Japanese people thought so.

Japan was a culture obsessed with size. Everyone, men and women alike, was concerned with staying skinny. The Japanese people seemed to be genetically slight, but in that culture people made comments about each other's weight in passing conversation.

If you expected a, "Hi, how are you?" you were more likely to get "You lost weight?" My internal response was usually, "Thanks a lot. I'm glad I'm not the gross hippo I used to be!" I was still trying to get used to it.

Worse, as hostesses, our job was to collect business cards, like a kid collected baseball cards, the more the better. And the day after we got them, we were expected to call the guy and drone on, "Hey, so-and-so, nice meeting you last night at Mikey's! I had an awesome time! Let's do it again! Call me."

We had to call more than ten people with the same message every day. Some would hang up on us, or say they were in a meeting. Some would not remember. It was not flattering to the old ego.

But the nightly meetings before the customers arrived were the worst part of all. We had to show Mikey our nails, stockings and makeup before we could clock in. Then Mikey would breeze in and begin a long-winded explanation in Japanese about the same shit he said the night before.

Huge Hair would translate, "get the name cards, call the customers, and get *dohans*." An enormous sign hung in The Dungeon, naming the girls in numerical order: Natasha, etc., blah, blah, blah. Then he would find some new Eastern European or non-English, non-Japanese speaking, vulnerable girl to pick on, asking to see her notebook.

We had to keep a record of all custies we sat with and their phone numbers, every *dohan* and requests and all custies we called each day. We had to leave the notebooks in a safe at the club each night, for fear of the police finding them if they checked us.

Of course, the poor new girl would not have many entries in her book, being fresh off the boat, and Mikey loved that. He would tear into her, saying things that were translated into, "Try harder! Be more like Natasha! Put more makeup on!" He never picked on girls from native English speaking countries, realizing we would (and could) get up and walk out. He took his frustrations out on those poor girls, and it was getting harder for me to bite my tongue.

I would not be quiet for long. I was commencing with "Phase Two," and I was bringing as many girls with me as I could convince to come with me. Phase Two involved a new club, "Jack's." Shishi took me there as a treat the week before. Instead of going to our usual sumptuous dinner, I was greeted by a debonair, yet innocent grin only Shishi could have pulled off. He promised me the experience of being a custie myself.

The opulence and drama of Jack's intrigued me straight away. The club was colossal, with humungous red velvet couches flanking black cement walls, adding flair to the smoky atmosphere. Hip-hop music played, instead of the usual folk classics that were prominent background music at Mikey's. Stunning women were everywhere, flirting. There was a stage, with a sassy cabaret show in progress, and there were easily twenty waiters bustling about with trays, laden with bottles of bubbly.

Shishi introduced me to the manager, a brusque, half Japanese man who turned out to have the same birthday as me. Shishi said that anyone who was anyone coming to Tokyo came in to Jack's. Britney Spears was there the week before and had been indulgent when the dancers performed their version of *Hit Me Baby, One More Time*. It seemed so laidback there. There was no nightly meeting and there were sixty or more other hostesses from all over the world. It was my club!

According to my plan, the day after I received my salary, I was going to go "Jerry McGuire" on their asses. I was going to wait until he started his a rampage on some poor girl, and then I was going to stand calmly, tell him how disgraceful he was, quit and say, "Who's coming with me?" I loved my new plan. It made the next week seem bearable.

I had already found accommodations through a slumlord named Pin. It was a filthy, junk-filled box of an apartment, with a miniscule bathroom, for around thirteen hundred Canadian dollars a month. It was my only option, if I didn't want to spend ten grand on a deposit for a "real" apartment in Japan. There were many people who wondered how we could live in such crowded conditions, in virtual squalor. It sounded awful. And yes, parts of it *were* awful, but our options were limited.

Most girls at the club were extremely intelligent and have had some sort of higher education. Most, like the good girls that they had been brought up to be, went to college straight after school and got their Bachelor of Arts Degree or another degree. Many were saddled with enormous debt in the form of student loans. Every girl I knew had started jobs in the work force, fresh faced and positive, only to be struck down by reality.

We were the working poor. We earned enough money to barely survive. We could pay our rent, buy food and make our student loan payments, but that was it. The price we had to pay to earn more money was simple, yet horrifying. That price was our youth. Anyone who put ten years into a job that they loathed might see a change in their bank accounts. But by that time, they would be thirty-five, having wasted their youth working their asses off.

It was even worse for the girls who worked in poor countries. They would never have enough money to broaden their minds and opportunities, working for pennies a day, never able to save for their dreams. Hostess work helped to support their families back at home, many of whom still lived in poverty.

The young women I met at Mikey's wanted more. They had dreams. They were not content to sit by and continue to be the working poor. Hope and youth were a powerful combination. It was the reason they could put up with working as hostesses. If they saved their money on a three month stint as a hostess, they could earn one important advantage their countries could never provide: the freedom to do what they willed.

MARYS AND WEED JESUS

Two days before payday and Phase Two, I got bitchy. My period had synched with almost every woman in our crowded abode, and I just ran out of weed. My favorite hangout was the tiny table in the center of the room where we cooked, ate, got ready, called custies and chatted.

I was in a foul mood for two reasons: one, I had not seen Ryu since the night Sato-san got pissed off at Natasha, though he was still haunting my dreams; and two, I had lost Hiro-Elvis as a regular good custie. I hadn't seen or heard from him since the *dohan*, when he gave me the watch.

Weeks went by. And then, the night before, he had waltzed into the club, in typical Hiro-Elvis fashion, flashing a blonde Russian, who looked about twelve. Every girl got to sit with him, except me. I had to sit in the Dog Box alone.

"Why did I lose him?" I asked the girls.

Apparently, he liked girls just fresh off the boat, naive and easy to get drunk. I appeared to be his type that first night with my horrid dress, timid drinking and awful *karaoke*. How flattering! *Why would he like such a girl?* Simply: sex. The world revolved around sex. I was not saying it was only men, because I was a fiend!

Hiro-Elvis wanted to get laid, and that task was a lot easier preying on vulnerable, desperate women. He could have gone to a prostitute, but paying for sex took away the chase. It was easier to host private parties, where he was the center of attention, where he might get a naive girl to fall for his charms.

He always needed to be the center of attention, and he was cunning with his larger than life thunder. Over time, he grew bored with me. Hiding behind dark sunglasses, he secretly checked out the other hostesses at the table. He sized them up for possible dinner companions and smiled his charming, fickle smile.

I didn't really blame him. If I were him, and I frequented hostess clubs, I would want ten hot guys surrounding me, telling me how great I was, vying for my attention in hopes of going on a date with me. I had to admit it sounded appealing.

Yet I learned from the Hiro-Elvis situation. First, that though our run was brief, it was profitable and gave me a sense of accomplishment. Second, it made me vow to be pickier about customers. It was important to surround myself with interesting, stimulating people.

It was tempting to become false, to become the perfect girl for every customer in every situation. I would make oodles of dough. But it was too draining and I was too lazy for such nonsense. I had a feeling that wonderful, like minded customers would find me. They had to be out there.

I had given up fantasies of finding my pseudo twin in the club. Sapphire and Diamond were best friends, though I sometimes forced myself on them. One night, I went to the fridge after curfew call to get a snack. I was disappointed by the weak display there: seaweed, dried squid/cheese and the sourest pickled plums I had ever tasted. When I turned from the fridge, I saw a blonde, headed out the door.

"Sapphire?" I asked, surprised to see her.

"Oh! How you going, Rose?" she asked, nervous, like she was in an interrogation chamber.

"On your way out?" I asked, prying.

"Oh, all *right*! I'm on my way over to Takeshi's. I can't keep a secret to save my life. I honestly wasn't really attracted to Asian men before, but God, he's so good in bed! It's not true about their dicks either, you know." She had told me that before, but I had first-hand knowledge. What a shock that was. Sapphire was actually dating Huge Hair!

"He seems so jaded and stand-offish," I commented.

"It's all an act," she replied, "He is a bit of a challenge, but all men are. Let's talk later. Don't tell anyone."

The next afternoon, I was sitting at the table with Tiffany, when a tall, gorgeous blonde man burst into the room to pick Tiffany up.

"Justin!" she screeched, turning white. "What are you doing here?"

"I wanted to surprise you, Baby. Get ready, and let's go out for some sushi! I checked us into a great hotel." He swung her around, knocking over furniture.

She was screwed and she knew it, but her dazzling hostess smile never failed. She was working as a hostess, but he thought she was a model. And she was already going for sushi with a man called

Tokyo Gigolo. Besides, she had to abide the five a.m. curfew or lose five hundred dollars. At a loss for words, she stumbled into our shared room and mumbled something incoherent.

If nothing else, I'm a brilliant schemer. I followed her into the room, sat her down and told her my plan. She would tell Justin she had to go to an audition and ask him to wait at the Starbucks near our house. Then she would go to the *dohan* with TG, get him to leave early, and pretend to be deathly ill.

Calling in sick at Mikey's was out of the question. Getting out of work required us to physically go in and show management how pathetic and sick we really were. After an Oscar caliber performance, Tiffany was free to go off with Justin, and I would take the curfew call as British and deathly ill Tiff.

We prayed that the club would not send someone to the apartment to check on her. The next afternoon, she would tell Justin that she was busy in the evening. Then she would go to work, collect her salary, join my Jerry McGuire team and move in with me.

"Brilliant!" she exclaimed as she became herself again. She motored around the room, trying on different outfits. I still had not solved my weed problem when I asked Tiffany if she knew of anyone who sold weed.

"Svetlana dates Weed Jesus. Ask her."

Svetlana? Hey! I had not thought of her since that first night. She was a loner who kept to herself, unlike me. I did not know it at the time, but the decision to contact Svetlana would change the course of my life and my destiny in Japan.

As fate would have it, I did not even have to call her. As I walked down the main street of Azabu Juban, basking in the late afternoon sun, lost in daydreams, Svetlana stood in front of me, exuding positive energy.

"I knew I'd see you today like this," she stated, unemotional. "Come with me."

I wondered if Tiffany told her about my quest for weed. I had not spoken more than a couple of sentences to Svetlana during the entire time I had been in Japan, and yet she was acting as if we had known each other for a millennium.

She did not utter another word until we arrived at an old apartment building and went up the stairs. I had not noticed it earlier, but even without a stitch of makeup Svetlana was beautiful, remarkable! She had deep-set, lavender eyes that reflected an ambivalence, which left me feeling confused. She was tall, six feet without heels, and lithe, like a ballerina. I had to hurry to keep up with her strides as we climbed the stairs.

In contrast to bravado and comedy, Svetlana was a woman of few words, and the words she spoke seemed well contemplated. I had a vision of clarity. I knew at once I had found my pseudo twin.

We arrived at Weed Jesus' apartment. It was saggy and battered, consisting of three rooms. Two were reserved for friends who fell on hard times. In any given week, there could be an assortment of people staying in the rooms. When I entered, one room was occupied by a French girl and her two-year-old daughter. Both were covered with a strange skin disease, with pustules. The girl could not get night work because she could not pay for someone to look after her daughter.

The other room was occupied by an Israeli guy hiding out because he had overstayed his visa. He was a funny, dark little fellow named Rory, who was always coming up with ideas to scam the Japanese government. For example, he would blurt out, "What if I got some really cheap drugs imported from Israel, sold it to someone and had enough money to buy a new passport?" I found some of his ideas interesting.

I never understood why I enjoyed socially unacceptable behavior, living on the edge or sticking it to "The Man." It started when I was a kid. When I was five, I admired the handiwork of my parents' friend, who had created a motorcycle out of bones. I was not scared. I was not freaked out at all. On the contrary, it intrigued me in the same way I was fascinated by the sound of a tattoo needle, drilling and pumping mini Picassos into the skin of the willing.

I felt comfortable at the apartment, and Jesus turned out to be one of the most charismatic, friendly and sensitive guys I had ever met. He was a handsome, muscular Iranian man. I had seen him before in Roppongi, usually accompanied by beautiful women.

He had numerous aliases, but his close friends called him "Jesus." To me he resembled Jesus, with flowing auburn hair and a kind and good aura. We sat together and discussed important issues, such as music and books, Roppongi craziness and world culture.

"How'd you two meet, anyway?" I asked Svetlana.

"I was sitting in a park near here, smoking and relaxing one day. I was playing with my figurine, watching the sun glint off her back," she answered. From her pocket, she took a small pewter figurine of a female cat. "When I looked down at my figurine, she had a message for me. 'In front of you,' the figurine said, and I when looked up, there was Jesus, watching me intently. As soon as I spotted him, he approached me. Upon spotting my figurine, he laughed, surprised, and pulled out the same figurine from his own pocket, yet his was a male cat. The rest is history."

As I got to know Svetlana better, I understood and accepted her psychic visions. She was a spiritually powerful woman. Her parents were teachers, and every night after she finished her regular homework, her parents made her study an extra hour of English, so she was a fluent speaker.

I told them about Canada and about growing up on a farm in the subarctic central region. We had an ice skating rink in the backyard that my dad made by flooding the yard with a water hose. We rode wild horses bareback all summer. I even rode them standing up. Svetlana and Jesus got a kick out of that.

Jesus' stories about Iran were bittersweet and revolved around wars and losing loved ones to atrocities. His family was gone, with the exception of his mother, who lived alone in a small community. His two brothers died in battles, serving their mandatory, army service requirements. His sister was disowned after being accused of adultery. She had an affair. It was her first offense and cost her family and respect.

As punishment, she was given one hundred lashes. In shame, she committed suicide. Under Islamic law, a third offense would have caused her to be buried with her head and neck above ground while her peers stoned her to death.

I wondered what the people of Islam would have thought about the hostess industry. I was sure they would have seen it as a shameful occupation, but men were men. Regardless of culture, men would always find ways to cavort with women. And in that culture, a man could have as many as four wives and could legally commit adultery without dishonoring his family.

When Svetlana's turn came to speak about her life and place of birth, she twirled her long hair and gazed at the floor. As a young girl, she grew up in the former Czechoslovakia. I thought she was Russian because she spoke the language fluently. She had not corrected my assumption because she wanted to know me before sharing her personal life.

When she spoke of the former Czechoslovakia, it was about communism. She never had oranges or chocolate before communism was eradicated, and her family had to ration toilet paper. Her parents were brilliant artists, but they could not leave Czechoslovakia to promote or sell their work.

Frustrated, her parents were distant and cold to their sensitive, only child. Svetlana grew up painting dreary landscapes and was thankful for the modeling contracts that allowed her an escape. After communism was abolished, she enjoyed traveling and meeting people, but she was unfulfilled.

She did not trust any industry where she had to use her looks and body to get ahead. "I won't sell my soul for a Gucci bag," she told me time and again. "I knew we were to be friends," she confided. "I saw your aura the first day that you came and started a painting of you." I was flattered. She said my aura was green and purple.

As we left, Jesus told me to come by anytime I was in the area (my house was a five minute walk away), just for a chat or to get some weed. Weed Jesus left me with a wise piece of advice regarding my chosen job. "Get yourself a Mary," he recommended. *What the hell was a Mary?* I wondered. I still had so much to learn about being a hostess.

The next day, I had the unpleasant task of lying to my mother, straight up. "No Mom, the bartending is great here and I've started English teaching. I'm living with stable people and I'm not partying too much." Diamond nodded to me as she made a similar reassurance to her mother by phone.

In reality, everyone there, myself included, lied to their parents about to their jobs. Television documentaries painted a seedy picture of those clubs. No one wanted to age their parents prematurely by telling them the truth. Not to mention, if people back home knew what we did in Japan, they would call us prostitutes. We just wanted to make our money and go home with respect.

It was noon, and I had been awakened by the same dream in which Ryu pushed me off the cliff, but I was getting used to it. I wanted to make more of my journey to Japan. There had to be more than mere financial gain. I would have money for CD costs, but that wasn't enough for me. It meant I had settled, choosing to wait for money rather than to pursue my dreams.

I loved to sing and write music, but the schedule I had and the life I led made it hard to concentrate on writing anything. There was not enough time or space, with constant hostess duties and crowded accommodations. I had to have a realistic nonmonetary goal. I did not want to look back on my time as having been wasted.

That night was Natasha's *sayonara* party, salary day and the beginning of Phase Two. Maybe it would be the beginning of my destiny with Svetlana. I was ready for it. Later that night, we all sat in the Dog Box, revelling that we could talk without management breathing down our necks.

"Did you hear the new rule?" Diamond cackled. "It's hysterical. We are not allowed to wear our hair up anymore because Mikey reckons... get this – that having our hair up makes us look like we are getting ready to give the custie a blow job." We roared as Mikey came out to start the dull ass meeting that would be the last I would suffer through.

The night turned out to be great in terms of A-Requests and custies coming in to see me. First, Shishi came in and livened up the club with his usual party atmosphere, accompanied by "Shishi Specials," which were a cloying and lethal combination of liquors. Over time, the night became a blur.

Hiro-Depp came in around one a.m. and just shuffled over to his dark corner table without looking at anyone. Gloomy, he nursed a whiskey and water on the rocks. He always looked a little nonchalant, but he seemed downright grumpy that night. I sat next to him.

"What's up Hiro?" I asked, bored.

He ignored me, still sipping. He was being a baby and it got on my nerves. I had a warm booze buzz going and he was killing it. I also had tons of other tables needing my attention.

"I'm outie." I stood and stalked over to Mikey in front of the club, and I asked him to move me to another table.

Both Mikey and Hiro-Depp were shocked that I decided to move myself because it just was not done. Hostesses were expected to comply with everything customers demanded. But I had authority issues. That, combined with the euphoria I felt about it being my last night at the club, made me feel invincible.

There was nothing they could do to punish me. They could not force me to sit at the table if I did not want to. We had a stare down, which I won easily while discovering my advantage. I, or should I say we, as hostesses, were the most valuable assets in the club, and we would do well to remember that.

It was a valuable lesson I would carry in my future as a businesswoman if I was going to succeed in that job. When Mikey conceded, he ushered me to a corner on the right and whispered into my ear, "A-Request."

He directed me to a red velvet alcove, the most private in the club, as it was partially hidden by the *karaoke* machine. Who should I see seated there, but Ryu! I could not believe my luck. We were about to speak our first words to one another.

As I rounded the corner, I recognized the stooped figure of an old man with glasses on. Sato-san had an energy surrounding him that made people want to bask. Since Natasha was leaving and he was pissed off at her, I guessed he wanted to meet the other girls.

I could feel eyes boring into the back of my head, and I knew they were Natasha's. I felt pity for her because I knew that she was in love with Sato. I tried not to appear too eager to meet him, hoping to ease her suffering.

I had found the dirt on Sato-san just the week before. Supposedly, he was the one who signed our pay checks, the head honcho. Hostesses were not supposed to know that. I did not know why, but I was not about to discuss it with him that night.

No one knew where he got his money, but he was definitely loaded and he loved to spend money on hostesses and on any kind of gambling, especially horse racing. He was a strange man who could take a liking to a girl or despise her for arbitrary reasons.

He spoke perfect English, and from what I gathered, he was a shrewd individual. I planned on leaving the club, but something told me Sato-san would be a valuable contact. Sato-san introduced himself and Ryu and smiled in a distracted way as I introduced myself. I was peeved that Ryu had not acknowledged me or spoken to me, let alone looked me in the eye.

After my *shiro* wine came, I lifted my glass for a toast and noticed they were both drinking hot tea. Sato-san had a few small, medicine bottles in front of him.

"To good health!" I offered.

Surprised, Sato-san looked up and asked me where I was from. Mikey had already told him I was Canadian, but as we spoke, he relaxed and began listing off his ailments. He was afflicted with everything from hay fever, to high blood pressure, to kidney stones and arthritis. He was the epitome of a hypochondriac and seemed excited as he detailed his symptoms.

"What I really need is a hand massage," he hinted.

I balked at the suggestion of such an intimate gesture, but I decided to go with the flow. I took his swollen, soft red hand in mine and began kneading the heel of his palm. Soon he fell asleep and began snoring softly, a happy smile on his face. It was almost three a.m., closing time. I was surprised again at the speed at which most Japanese people could fall asleep.

A chill ran down my spine as I turned to see Natasha, staring at us with a look that could kill. Looking down at Sato-san's hand still in mine, I realized it looked like we were holding hands. She was not the first to fall head over heels for the power figure in the club. It was not a rare phenomenon.

Many girls from various countries had fallen for his charms, the most notorious being a girl who threatened to slit her wrists when his interest waned. She had to be shipped back to a loony bin in her country. Feeling sorry for Natasha, I broke Sato's grip and waved to her. She did not return the gesture.

The night was about to end and I wanted to speak to Ryu, but I was running out of time. I leaned over, touched Ryu's chest gently and breathed into his ear, "You're so sexy." He didn't flinch as he returned my gaze. I wasn't sure what I saw in his eyes, whether it was lust or disgust. At last, I was the one to wimp out and look away, though still he had not spoken to me.

I was proud of myself for making the first move, however intoxicated I was. I would have never had the courage to approach him like that without being a little drunk. When the lights came up and I looked around the club, I noticed all the custies had left and it was time for our nightly meeting. For once, Mikey did not rush me around to see all the customers off at the elevator.

I excused myself to the washroom to gather what was left of my dignity. My brief encounter with Ryu left me devastated. There were two restrooms. One shabby little hole was reserved for the use of hostess bums, and a larger restroom with an ornate mirror and a fresh bouquet of flowers was for the customers. We were not supposed to use the customer's toilet, but I was not in the mood.

I slipped into the room, smiling, and was surprised. The usually bubbly Sapphire was seated on the small counter, trying in vain to control her tears, while Diamond patted her back. It was useless trying to console her.

"Takeshi's been fired. Waiters aren't allowed to date hostesses," she moaned.

Sapphire was loved in our house. She and Diamond were wonderful roommates. I really cared about them. The rules being enforced by the Roppongi Gestapo were hurting my friends.

"Screw them!" I fumed. "Come work with me at Jack's. I'm going to get my salary tonight and kiss this place goodbye. As it is, I'm already taking Svetlana and Tiffany. If you guys leave, they will be losing five of their best hostesses," I reasoned.

"Done. I can't stand this place anyway," Sapphire sneered, wiping her tears and reapplying her war paint.

"Good call, Rose!" Diamond chimed in, adjusting her raven curls with a graceful twist of her wrist.

"I'm taking all my Marys with me," Diamond declared.

"What's a Mary?" I asked. It was the second time I heard the word.

"A Mary is a generous customer with astronomical wealth," Diamond answered.

"Why the word Mary?" I was curious.

"A while ago, Diamond was meeting a custie called Polly, short for The Politician," Sapphire answered, "and I asked her what his real name was. She was like, 'I have no idea. He could be called Mary for all I care, as long as he's got a black Amex.' It just kind of stuck. We use it more like a code word now. We whisper it under our breath when we see a custie that fits the bill."

When we finished our conversation, we walked out of the restroom, determined, and took our seats in the Dog Box. The time had come to set The Man straight and regain our independence. We were going to teach them a lesson in respect.

PHASE TWO

Natasha's slender six-foot frame trembled behind an enormous bouquet of roses as tears streamed down her gorgeous face. "I vill miss you all," she wailed. "I said that I vould not cry. Good luck to all new girls." She looked like the winner of a beauty pageant in an alternate universe. We all grabbed her in a farewell hug and clustered together for a group photo shot. What a picture that would make!

The walls of the Dungeon were covered with hundreds of similar pictures from years back. They featured young women from all over, wearing provocative dresses and gaudy high heels. There were many peroxide blondes, suntanned bodybuilders, exotic, dark women with incredible figures and subdued, contemplative girls who would not smile.

The photos were proof that we existed in a world where we were supposed to be kept hidden. They represented another misconception about hostess clubs. Everyone saw the girls in the club as generic, but we were individuals. We were unique in terms of personalities, hopes, culture and character.

That was why customers continued to frequent the clubs year after year. They were always looking for something or someone new and different. The girls were forever changing and moving, and that was part of the appeal.

Mikey's had been open for years, since the infamous Japanese "Bubble Economy" that had blessed the hostess world. It spanned three glorious decades before abruptly ending in the late 1980s. I had heard fairy tales and whispered stories about girls getting condos, new cars and unlimited scores of free flowing cash.

But back to the present and the calm before the storm – shit went down at club Mikey's that night. The good news was Natasha felt better and was going home with a big wad of cash. She had forgotten about Sato-san and seemed to have shaken her obsession with him. She got a grip when faced with the realization that she would be on a flight back to Russia within a few hours, much richer than she had arrived.

We did not get along initially, but I saw beauty in her, in her loyalty and in her direct manner. I could not judge her. I did not know much about Russia, the country, its history or its culture. Natasha's story was more complex than it seemed. She was working to support her family and herself.

One thing I had noticed: the Russian and Eastern European girls were discriminated against in Roppongi, and the mistreatment began the moment they reached Narita airport. They had a harder time getting into the country. Because their own countries were poor, airport officials thought they would engage in illegal activities through necessity. Those girls were denied the standard three month tourist visas upon entry, all for being from the wrong country.

The club, if management sensed desperation in a girl, would use it to their advantage. And customers would treat desperate girls differently by acting more scabby or trying to get away with being revolting. Svetlana told me many sad stories about being discriminated against.

The Eastern European girls were paid half our salary. We all received airfare, accommodations, weekly and monthly bonuses, which were calculated, based on the number of *dohans* and A-Requests we had. But I was getting a monthly wage of ¥320,000, about thirty-two hundred dollars, while they were getting paid ¥160,000 per month. It was unfair.

I am not patriotic. I had developed a patriotic illness that could only be cured by culture. I was proud to be from Canada, though. Along with its stunning beauty, it also boasted multiculturalism, freedom of expression, free health care and democracy.

When we got paid our wages, I found out the club had kept half of my money, which they would hold until my contract was finished two months later. They did the same to Svetlana, because she had started a week prior to me. So she only had around eight hundred dollars after working her ass off for a month. What a joke!

The girls scrambled toward The Dungeon to retrieve their belongings and to change their clothes after the meeting was presumed to be over. "I have something to say," I started, with all eyes on me. "Mikey, I think that your treatment of us is awful and we are leaving – Svetlana, Tiffany, Sapphire, Diamond and me." It was so nice to see him squirm for once.

"What?" Mikey stuttered in a rage. "What about your contract?"

"Wasn't that why you kept half my wages? That money should cover my ticket cost. You're a rude little man and I can't stand watching you treat people like shit for another minute. C'mon girls. Let's jet!" I started for the door. For once, the other hostesses stood back and let us grab our stuff first.

Mikey was livid as he screamed at us, "You have to be out of the apartment tonight!"

"That's fine!" I snapped back. I had already seen it coming, as I heard from another hostess about Mikey throwing one poor girl out in the middle of the night. It had turned into a physical fight, including karate kicks down the staircase. It had all ended in blood, on Mikey's part, as the girl was quite a fighter.

I had already secured the apartment earlier in the week from the slumlord, Pin. He was a slimy, stinky character, who had subtly tried to hit on me while his wife and kid waited in the car. It was one of the foulest apartments I had ever seen, with its dirty, clinical blue walls. It was a ghetto pad that had fifty-year-old carpets. When I found a used condom under the bed on move in day, I was not surprised. And he had the cheek to charge us a cleaning fee!

We strutted out of there together, walking arm in arm, savoring in our victory. We were free! Mikey had been power-hungry and unkind. What he hadn't expected was our fearlessness. He understood too late that we were essential to the club and would probably take their top customers with us. Regardless, we won against the management. It was a taste of power in the form of kicking them where it hurts... in the wallet.

MAMMA-SAN

Tiffany had loaded our suitcases in a taxi to Akasaka and our new apartment. We had all packed the night before and were quick in our flight from the AZABU TOWERS hostess apartment. My phone was ringing off the hook, though I didn't bother to answer it. It started up again and I ignored it. Even if Mikey was on the other end, groveling to get us back, I didn't want to hear it. I would leave the borrowed phone too, when I left.

All of a sudden, a black BMW, with blacked out windows, pulled in front of the taxi, and a dark figure emerged. Sato-san approached me with an unhappy glint in his eye. "Rose. Can I speak with you?" He gestured toward the black automobile, waiting.

I was taking a great risk. I had been told never to get into a car with a customer. But my gut told me that it wasn't really a request on Sato-san's part. It was more of a command. Instinctively I sensed he would not harm me. I turned to see Tiffany staring at me, her aquamarine eyes filled with dread.

"Go to the new apartment with our bags, and I will meet you there later," I told her, with an easy smile to calm her nerves. She nodded slowly, gave me another apprehensive look, and climbed into the taxi, pulling her sunglasses low, down over her nose.

Sato-san waited until I was in the backseat before he joined me. He leaned toward the driver and grumbled his desired location in succinct Japanese. The driver nodded his bald, scarred head, his gigantic glasses bouncing up and down on his small, crumpled nose.

We drove for a few minutes in silence until we came upon an ancient Japanese cafe that was open at four a.m. The proprietor was a tiny, stooped woman, dressed in a grey kimono. She seemed ecstatic when Sato-san and I entered. There were no other customers in the old-fashioned room.

As our oolong tea came, I was the one to break the silence. "So, what do you want?" I was trying to be straightforward. It seemed he was trying to intimidate me, and it was working. But it would take more than that to make me lose hold of my convictions.

Just then a tall, familiar man burst through the doors and approached our table, seating his lanky frame across from me. When he removed his glasses, I realized it was Ryu. "What do you think you are doing?" he demanded.

What romantic first words, I thought, sarcastically. "Oh. You *can* speak?" I was enjoying egging him on.

"Of course I can speak," he spat. "What is the meaning of the girls leaving the club? *Baka!*" I knew that *baka* basically meant stupid.

"What is the meaning of all the *baka* rules in the club, then?" I retorted. "We're being treated like second class citizens, and we won't stand for it anymore."

As Ryu began to argue with me again, Sato-san spoke to me in a gentle voice. "Can you tell us what is so unbearable?"

I was surprised he was so calm, but I could still see that glint in his eye, and I sensed danger. I took a deep breath and started to detail the most demeaning and unbearable club rules and regulations.

"First," I answered, "there are the meetings and ridiculous rules which do nothing but bring the morale of the girls down. That is unproductive for you as businessmen. Those meetings should be used to discuss how we can get more customers, or to address girls who were having problems – not to weigh us every week and put us down."

I waited for a response, but none came, so I continued, "Next, there is the fact that we can make more money at Jack's, and every girl is paid the same wage, no matter what country she is from. And lastly, there is the fact that Takeshi's been fired, for no other reason than falling in love." I hurried to finish so I wouldn't lose my nerve.

The two men began speaking in staccato Japanese. As they discussed the topic, I began to comprehend the situation that I was in. I was dealing with the *Yakuza*. I had heard many stories about the underground mafia in Japan. I had expected tattooed hooligans, who would be easy to distinguish from other people on the street. Those two looked so normal.

Weed Jesus dealt with the mafia and said they ran all of Japan, including Roppongi. They had control over everything, from banks to construction companies, and sometimes even police. I knew that when we left the club, Sato-san might be a bit put out, but I had no clue he was mafia and that he would take such a personal interest in where we worked. I wasn't keen on being labeled as someone else's property.

When I looked up, they were both staring at me, silent.

"We have decided that you stay at Mikey's and become *Mamma-san*," Sato-san announced.

"No way! That place sucks my spirit." I leveled a steady gaze and took a deep breath.

"You know *mamma-san* can change things, can help people," Ryu tried. He knew that would make me think.

"What does a *mamma-san* do?" I asked, suspicious.

"It is a very important job. You help new girls understand the industry. You control the atmosphere of a club." Sato-san was a good salesman.

"No thanks. I don't want the responsibility." I was meant to be at a fun loving, tolerant club like Jack's.

"We would consider this a favor, and we would be grateful. We would also double your wages and give you added benefits, like paying your phone bills and apartment." Sato-san acted as if he had already sealed the deal.

I hesitated. My goal was to go home with ten thousand dollars. *What if I could double that amount and also make a few more girls' lives more bearable for the three month period?* I also understood that Sato-san was a man who got what he wanted, and I realized his request was a command.

"What about Takeshi?" I did not want to stay at Mikey's, not without Sapphire and Diamond, and they would have never stayed there without Takeshi.

After taking a deep breath, Ryu looked into my eyes and said, "That is not a rule that can be changed at Mikey's, ever. Staff members can never date."

"Well, Diamond and Sapphire will not be staying at the club. You will lose two really good hostesses." I was trying to barter as well.

"*Shoganai*," Sato-san said, impatient. I knew the expression meant, "That's life."

"Will you raise the salaries of the other eastern European girls?" I asked. I would have rather died than watch Svetlana make a lesser wage for the same job.

"Yes. We will put all the girls on a percentage system. The more customers they have, the more money they will make. Everyone will be able to earn the same basic monthly wage of ¥320,000 per month. For someone like Svetlana, who has several customers, she can earn a lot more." He already knew how much I loved her. I contemplated that change to my plans and weighed the consequences.

"I agree to your terms, and I will start as *mamma-san* tomorrow night." I knew that they would not take "no" for an answer, and I was excited to change things at Mikey's. In reality, I had entered into a deal with the mafia and created a hostess union, of sorts. After the meeting was over, I got out of there fast. I called Tiffany the moment I got back to the hostess apartment and filled her in on what the meeting entailed for me.

I knew that she would join the Aussies at Jack's and that they would have an absolute blast. I was happy for them, but it wouldn't be the same at the club without them. Jack's would be a lot better for Tiffany, because she was still hiding her job from Justin. It made sense for them, and I hoped that my future would bring clarity as well.

"Do you think I made the right choice?" I asked Tiffany.

"Did you *have* a choice?" she answered.

That night, I was dead asleep when Ryu pulled another "B&E" into my universe of dreams. *Reaching toward me, his gentle, playful eyes were bright with humor. I wouldn't fall for that again. I leaned toward him, and when he was least expecting it, I tackled him off the cliff and grabbed him in my arms as we plunged downward, laughing into each other's eyes. I leaned over to kiss his sensual lips and...*

Ring, ring, ring. My irritating phone would not stop ringing. I wanted the dream to continue. I tried to return, to no avail. I peeked out from beneath my sleeping mask and glanced at the clock, which read 3:37 p.m.

Who the hell was calling me when I wasn't in the mood? After a glance at the bright orange screen, I realized Hiro-Depp had called me at least five times that day. *Whatever happened to playing hard to get?*

Ring, ring, ring. Oh God! Now it was Mikey harassing me.

"*Moshi Moshi*," I answered in a tired voice.

"*Mikey desu*. You meet Sato-san for dinner tonight at seven p.m. Meet him in front of the Wendy's Azabu Juban, and don't be late. I will come at your apartment soon. I give you something." I thought he was going to talk about the previous night.

"Okay," I answered with a tired voice.

Ring, ring, ring... I glanced at the caller ID and noticed Hiro-Depp's number showing up on my phone again. God, he was a persistent man!

"*Moshi Moshi*," I answered in my limited Japanese.

"Hi. Can you meet me on Sunday around three o'clock?" he asked. "I want to take you to a Japanese *onsen*. A hot springs!" He was out of breath, like he had been running. I was getting kind of bored with The Depp, but a hot springs excursion sounded like exactly what I needed. I had only been there for a month, but I was already drained. I was sick of the love/hate relationship I had with Ryu.

"Okay, sure," I sighed into the receiver. He hung up without a goodbye. I climbed back under my sheets and lied there, listening to the silence surrounding me. There used to be seven girls living there, but only Svetlana and I remained. It was a bit sad, even though we had a lot more space.

The first rule that I wanted to abolish was the curfew call. That would definitely result in Svetlana staying at Weed Jesus' house almost every night, which would leave me home alone. How strange!

My thoughts began to wander toward Ryu again. I wondered why I was I so infatuated. I didn't know anything about him. It was the first time I had been so smitten. But we were like oil and water. We did not get along at all. His actions the night before showed me as much.

Finally, I stopped spinning my thoughts, got out of bed and stepped into a hot shower. I hoped the water would wash away my confusion. I flipped the switch to my iPod and Bob Marley's familiar voice set my spirit at ease. Music was such medicine for me.

I chose my outfit for my *dohan* with Sato-san and decided on my favorite, lucky dress. It was my secret weapon of sorts. I zipped myself up into the tight, peach-colored, silk mini dress and felt like a million bucks. There was a slit up one thigh that allowed me to sit down. I was thankful for the slit, since the dress was skin-tight.

I sat down at the tiny kitchen table and curled my long blonde hair. I put on pearly peach lip gloss and smoky, grey eye shadow. *No Woman, No Cry* blared from the small speakers perched on my bedside table as I leaned out onto the tiny balcony to steal a toke.

All of a sudden, Mikey was knocking on my door, attired in his usual crisp suit. He carried a black gift bag with the word "Prada" on the outside. He held it out to me, without speaking. I had never owned anything designer, besides that watch from Hiro-Elvis. I had never even craved designer, but something in me changed as I unwrapped the gorgeous black Prada shoulder bag that Sato-san gave me.

The girls in the Dog Box made me feel a perverse sense of greed. I wasn't used to it, coming from a farm. The girls who had been there longer were always noticing other girls' designer handbags and commenting. "Did you see her Jimmy Choo?" they would gasp. I would reply with something like "Did she sneeze?" I had no idea that Jimmy Choo was a big name designer. People always wanted what other people had.

I wondered if Sato-san was trying to buy me. So what if he was. I knew I could never be bought, and it would take more than wealth to catch me in any web of monetary deceit. I would just try to enjoy the beautiful handbag and accept it as a reward. I tore the tags off and emptied my belongings into it, setting forth to meet Sato-san.

We went for *tepanyaki*, at a restaurant where a chef prepared the meal in front of us on an enormous metal grill. It was an eight course meal, consisting of asparagus, rolled in *taro* root and grilled tuna *sashimi* with soy sauce and *wasabi*, garlic rice, *miso* soup, pickles and tea to finish. It was hands down the best food I had ever eaten, and that was saying a lot, since I had dined at some truly magnificent restaurants in the amazing gourmet city of Tokyo.

Sato-san turned out to be a very entertaining dinner companion. He regaled me with tales of his boyhood, growing up in the countryside of Japan. It was just the two of us at the restaurant, with no sign of Ryu, which did not disappoint me. Ryu had turned me off with his aggressive and intimidating attitude.

The time with Sato-san flew by and I enjoyed myself. The last course before our roasted green tea was dessert. The fantastic chef sautéed succulent cherries in a high octane liqueur turned out the lights and set it on fire. The delicious fruit was topped with rich vanilla ice cream. I felt like those cherries, stewing in the hot, heady alcohol, ready to be enjoyed by a person who waited patiently and paid for the flavor.

HEAT SCORE

That night, I slept dreamless, grateful for the break from the visions that tormented me almost every night. Unfortunately, I also awoke with a blurred feeling, which was accompanied by a rough, dry stinky mouth. It was not a very pleasant way to start my morning (or afternoon).

I was glad no one could see me, as I was alone in the apartment. I focused my scratchy, uncooperative eyes on the clock, which read 4:20, so I immediately sparked up the fat roach on my bedside table. It was calling for me. When I recounted the previous night's events, a high-pitched chuckle escaped my lips.

Going on *dohan* with Sato-san secured my rank in the club, and the announcement of my promotion to *mamma-san* was the talk of the club. It felt weird in the club without Tiffany, Sapphire and Diamond livening things up, but I cured that with alcohol and insisted on having Svetlana at all my tables.

I would later be pulled into The Dungeon to examine photos of my friend's replacements. There were about five to ten photos from each agent, and we needed to choose five girls. Each agent was from a different country: Australia, England, Russia, Estonia, the US and Canada. I chose girls from the different photos: two Aussie girls, who were friends, two English girls and one girl from Estonia.

I knew I needed to balance the club out. The girls from countries where English was not the primary language tended to focus on Japanese customers and attracted a specific kind of client. Their ideal Mary's were older, loaded, conservative Japanese gentlemen. They had no interest in studying English.

The second category of customers could come in any form. Those clients could be Japanese or *gaijin*, they could be rich or poor, or they could be a president or a pretender. They were simply enamoured with meeting new people from different countries in order to experience new cultures. The majority of those custies also loved to *party*. They were not content sitting in the club in a non-committal way. They *were* the party, and each individual was unforgettable.

I prided myself on being able to woo both kinds of custies, but I preferred one with a bit of spice. Since we had the potential to spend a fair bit of time together, I insisted on custies who were generous and kind. If a custie was neither, I didn't give him the time of day.

Hiro-Depp came into the club on his best behavior and even surprised me by singing a sweet, yet somewhat tragic *enka* karaoke song. It was the first time I had heard him sing, and it surprised me how much his husky, scarred voice touched me.

I wasn't sitting with him because I had another request, but I asked the guy I was sitting with what the song meant. He told me Hiro-Depp's song was about waiting for the love of an untouchable woman.

When I finally sat with Hiro-Depp, he was just getting his check. Before he left he gave me one last searching look before whispering in my waiting ear, "I'm looking to Sunday, Rose."

I was looking forward to going to the *onsen* the next morning with him, but I was anticipating even more partying it up with my girls and hearing about their first night at Jack's. I was out the door before I knew it and met my friends at "The Crystal Lounge," a popular hangout and D.B. bar in Roppongi. I met them in the VIP area, which was a mirrored room with scarlet chandeliers and enormous *karaoke* screens everywhere.

A customer in the corner poured out his heart on the song, *The Green, Green Grass of Home*, in a mumbling, monotone twang. I also watched as his date poured out her glass of champagne into a nearby, abused and wilted tree. A three hundred dollar bottle of Veuve Clicquot sat in front of them on ice, like a trophy. I understood why she would choose to dump it out. She obviously wanted to order another bottle of Veuve, but she did not want to get too drunk. *Who knew how many gallons she already drank?*

"Sapphire! Diamond! Tiffany! And you must be... Justin!" I faltered on the last name. I was surprised to see Justin there. It was too close to our working territory to be good for any secrecy on Tiffany's part.

"The cat's out of the bag," Tiffany smiled. "He knows everything, Rose." Apparently, Tiff had a crisis that very day, in her typical fashion. While she had told Justin she was supposed to be at a fashion show, she was actually out to dinner with a custie called Yazzers.

They were on their way for D.B. *karaoke*, when they came across Justin. Of course, Tiffany was horrified and tried to duck into a nearby club, but Justin spotted her and made a huge scene in front of the famously busy Roppongi Crossing.

He ranted and raved, calling Yazzers a dirty old man and threatening to beat him to a pulp. Yazzers fled in a taxi, fearing for his life, and Tiffany was left with her heart on her sleeve and an armful of Gucci bags to explain. After a long, tearful night of explaining, Justin gave Tiffany a huge shock by being understanding and forgiving her. She got off with a warning of, "Let's just be honest with each other from now on."

Justin was one-of-a-kind. He was planning ways to help Tiffany earn more money and they were planning a trip to Thailand in the future. He decided to stay and accept what the cards had to offer. His eyes glowed with the light of night time Tokyo streets. He was hooked on the city.

Diamond was ecstatic with the news that she was getting six thousand dollars from a customer for her boob job. She was bold enough to ask and he said, "Yes." She felt like she had won the lottery. Nothing could bring her down from her high.

No one seemed to notice that Sapphire was not her usual self. She seemed to be in her own world and barely touched her champers. She also announced in a tired voice, "I've changed my mind about the boob job." That was strange, because when I first got to Mikey's, it was all she could talk about.

But I could see that my friend did not want to talk, so I left her to her own devices. We stayed in the Crystal Lounge for a couple hours and whooped it up. We even bought our own bottle of champagne, an unheard of feat for those whose salaries are derived from its consumption.

After a stop at the local *ramen* restaurant, we ended up in Quest, a huge club that never closed. I must have stumbled into a taxi and gotten my drunken ass home somehow. The last thing I remember was dancing on the bar with the girls, shaking our bodies to techno with a crowd of willing men surrounding us.

Diamond summoned me to the toilet a few minutes later and I was surprised to see her pull out a tiny baggie of coke from her bra. I could count on one hand the amount of times that I had done coke before, so I was initially apprehensive. I contemplated turning it down as we teetered on our heels, cooped up inside the small, filthy toilet. *Just one line won't hurt* I thought as I stuck the rolled up 10,000 yen note up my nose and sniffed the thin white line, straight to my already inebriated brain.

We sat there for a while in the cubicle and smoked a dube, which I had smuggled into the club in my bra. After we finished, I sprayed some perfume around the toilet, hoping to mask the strong smell. We were heat score.

Weed Jesus had warned me about that. He told me to be wary of cops, who could put a girl in jail for a month without even charging her. He told me scary deportation and bust stories and impressed upon me not to be a heat score by bringing weed out with me all the time. He was right and I knew it. I sighed and vowed to be better in the future.

When I woke up the next morning, I cursed myself for partying too hard, again. *How many times would I awake in a cloudy haze and not remember the previous night?* As I looked around the messy room for my robe, I heard the toilet flush and was horrified to find that I was not alone in the apartment.

Svetlana slept at Weed Jesus' apartment nightly, so I had gotten used to being alone in the mornings. I freaked out as I glanced to my right and noticed a pile of neatly stacked, male clothes, sitting on my chair. I did not know who they belonged to. They did not seem like Hiro-Depp's casual clothes.

What have you done? You slut! my inner voice screamed. A minute later, a dripping, wet, god of a man came into my room, as if he owned the place. He stood buck naked at the edge of my bed, his manhood on display. I tried to look anywhere but in front of me.

I did not know what was worse – the fact that Ryu was standing there or that all he wore was an enormous, smug, shit-eating grin.

"I guess... you no remember last night," he smiled. As he started to dress, I felt self-conscious in my own apartment. To make things worse, I had let the apartment turn into a hellhole. The whole place was in dire need of cleaning. My things were strewn about the apartment and the only thing in my fridge was crystal clear booze. It was embarrassing. I had no idea what to say to him.

"Are you going to tell me what happened last night?" I asked. "I thought you were so against staff relations." I did not know if we had sex. I looked down and realized I was wearing an elegant white, silk teddy that I had never worn before. In fact, I usually slept naked. I would have had to have been really drunk or daring to wear that outfit on a first night together. I did not know what had happened as I looked down to hide my blushing.

Stoic, he dressed, not speaking as he swaggered toward the door. He gave me one last look that was warm and yearning. As he was leaving, I had a flashback of him trying to dress me in the white teddy, while I retched into the kitchen sink.

"*Matta ne*, and yourself take care," he whispered in a concerned voice. He gestured toward the little roach remaining and the haze surrounding my bed. "Police are danger." And he was gone. He still had not answered my question about what the hell had happened the night before.

When I got up for a glass of water, I noticed that Ryu had cleaned my apartment! He had carefully folded my lingerie, piled my books and random papers in neat stacks on the kitchen table, and he washed the dishes.

On the tiny cubby used for cooking, there was a pot of delectable *miso* soup with turnips on the burner. I had not even noticed the pleasant, organic smell that filled the room. I was famished.

The nagging question that remained was, *had I slept with him?* I knew I was attracted to Ryu and I would have loved to have made my fantasies about him a reality, especially after he had cooked and cleaned for me. But he also pissed me off more than any other guy I had met.

He was naked, while I lied on the bed in skimpy lingerie. I smiled, adding that image to my series of daydreams about him. Before Japan, I did not have many lovers. I had one boyfriend most of my life. I definitely had sex on a regular basis, but with the same man. I knew him and his body well.

It had turned into a whole new game there in Japan. There was a sexy spirit, an undercurrent running rampant that captivated us all. I was a different woman in that Asian fantasy world. I was learning to see a dark, passionate side of me that I always knew existed, but never had the courage to show.

D.B. ROYALTY

I sat with Svetlana and Weed Jesus in Starbucks at Roppongi Crossing on a Friday night a few weeks later. We enjoyed ourselves as we sat drinking vanilla lattes, people watching and gossiping, like old ladies.

"I can't make enough money to start my art gallery in Prague before my visa expires." Svetlana sighed. She had confessed her dream to me in her shy way. She was careful with her money and kept an account of everything she made and spent. She had already saved ten thousand dollars, which she kept in a plastic bag in the freezer, but she had only a month to save another ten grand.

"Okay, let's solve that problem with a treasure hunt." I suggested. The girls, Diamond, Sapphire and Tiffany, were out every night making shitloads in drink back money. Svetlana and I either went out every night partying, or we went home and watched a movie and chilled. We would have to start a D.B. campaign to meet Svetlana's quota.

D.B.s, also known as Drink Backs, was a constant source of easy money. All we had to do was get custies to buy ridiculously expensive bottles of champagne or wine and sit around, singing *karaoke*. I was certain I could convince almost anyone to go if I wasn't being lazy. After the clubs ended, customers were buzzed, light hearted and easily swayed. I would target my richer clients. The bankers, CEOs and foreigners with expensive watches tended to be partiers who could afford to pay huge bills.

Diamond and Sapphire had gone out the night before and got thirteen bottles of Moët Chandon. One bottle cost four hundred dollars. They got fifty percent of that back, so two hundred dollars times thirteen bottles came to twenty-six hundred dollars for two girls. They were there for about four hours. There were not many jobs anywhere that paid three hundred dollars to unskilled employees.

Svetlana seemed pleased with my D.B. plan as she gave Weed Jesus a quick peck. We began to walk to work, revved up on our coffees and big dreams. I took one last glance at Weed Jesus and wondered what his night would be like. I bet he was lonely in the steamy streets as he sold drugs from between his balls, literally.

He was trying to make enough money to join Svetlana in Prague, so they could start a life together there.

I had lost Hiro-Depp, not only as a customer, but as a friend and lover too. The morning after Ryu stayed over, I was supposed to have met Hiro-Depp at Wendy's in Azabu Juban. We were supposed to go to the *onsen*, but I flaked on him.

I felt bad, but I knew that I could not keep seeing him, when I had such strong feelings for Ryu. After that, Hiro-Depp entered stalker territory, calling me a whopping twenty-six times in the three hours he waited. I had been in bed with Ryu all morning, not that I remembered it. I tried to call Hiro-Depp to apologize, but he was heartbroken and refused to answer my calls, let alone acknowledge me. When he came into the club, he requested to be seated with some new girls. It was a bittersweet loss for me.

I had not seen Sato-san or Ryu because they were in Australia on a business trip. Upon further investigation, I found out that Sato-san's "business" was to visit one of his girlfriends and possibly invest in a real estate venture she had put together. He was constantly getting calls from girls needing financial backing.

I missed all three men and tried to keep myself busy. The new hostesses had arrived, and it was up to me to show them the ropes. The blonde and bubbly Aussies were best friends. Kim was quite tall, with a thick frame, whereas Karla was petite. All the custies were enchanted by their accents, easy charm and stylish attire.

The English girl's name was Susan and she was every bit as blonde as the Aussies. She was a bit rougher and possessed a biting wit that kept us all in stitches. She earned the reputation of being able to drink anyone under the table, man or woman, Japanese or foreign.

She asked me where she could find coke on the first night she arrived and being the obliging *mamma-san*, I called up Weed Jesus and got him to deliver it to the back steps. After that, we snorted lines together almost every night. We even designated a secret place in the ladies toilet, where we could leave it for each other to brighten up a dull conversation at a boring table. I was glad that Ryu could not see me. I was often disgusted with myself in the morning.

I still had not found my rhythm in Roppongi. Every weekend, I tried to write music and tried to research how to promote myself. I felt productive. But I wanted to do something good in the club. I wanted my journey to have meaning.

When I met Lula from Estonia, my mission became apparent. She was a skinny and scared girl, whose brown, stringy hair hung down her bony shoulders. She stood slumping before me, unable to meet my gaze, utterly defeated. Her eyes, devoid of hope, touched my heart.

She did not trust me when I first sat down to explain her duties as a hostess, such as refilling dinks and ashtrays and selecting *karaoke* songs on the machine. It seemed she expected me to be next in her line of abusers.

It took weeks of kindness and patience for her to trust me enough to tell her heartbreaking story in broken English. Her father died before she was born. She was emaciated because her mother did not have enough money to feed her along with three siblings. Her younger sister had an illness that required an expensive and dangerous transplant.

Her older sister had been duped into taking a job in England, which forced her into prostitution. She returned with horror stories and a self-imposed need to protect her younger sisters. Lula was scarred from the stories and distrusted everything and everyone.

She had come to Roppongi in an act of desperation, as her younger sister's health deteriorated. Her family could not raise money for her ongoing medical expenses. They could barely afford to survive.

I would sit down with her every day, doing her makeup and helping her put outfits together. My clothes were too big for her, but the other girls were always willing to share clothes. Because we were the same shoe size, she just borrowed from my extensive and ever growing collection.

She had no sense of style, and for obvious reasons. She had not spent her youth reading fashion magazines and maxing out her parents' Visa card while shopping on the Internet. She struggled for her basic needs.

Nevertheless Lula, like all the other girls there, had a dream. She told me all she wanted was a house for her family – any house, anywhere. When she talked about her dream, her eyes would light up with an ethereal glow and take on a faraway quality.

"We would never leave that house," she said, fluttering. "We would be happy together. Yula would be fine." Yula was the name of her younger sister, who was ill –Yula and Lula.

I dreamed right along with her. We all did in that cramped little apartment, as if our collective energy could make good things happen. We all tried to find ways to be especially nice to Lula. I guess we must have felt a bit guilty, too. None of us *had* to be there. The rest of us were doing it for money and personal reasons.

I made sure I sent her to an amazing hair salon and I worked with her on poise and her English skills. I also shared fashion and makeup tips, which would be important if she wanted to attract generous and non-threatening custies. I was concerned about her safety. Svetlana, Weed Jesus and I were very protective of her.

And over time, she broke out of her shell. She began putting on weight, she walked with grace and confidence and she began to hold her head up high. The shy, reclusive girl I had met a few weeks before had blossomed into, a pretty, charismatic and witty woman. She became popular in the club and was adored by the customers. Her transformation was inspiring.

It made me feel good about myself. It felt good to help people, which gave me more of a purpose. That night, in accordance with my announced D.B. plan, some great D.B. customers waltzed through the doors only an hour before closing, ready to rage their *karaoke* skills.

Their names were Shin 1 and Shin 2. They were long lost twins who were separated at birth. Of course, they were affectionately known in the Dog Box circle as Stinky Shin and Gingivitis Shin, or B.O. Mary and Bad Breath Mary. Bad Breath Mary turned out to be a dentist, which was hard to believe.

They were nice, except that Gingivitis Shin kept trying to stuff one thousand yen notes down our bras after every song. They were always sweaty, yet harmless and always ready to have a good time. We had to develop a technique of breathing through our mouths at all times during and in between conversations, so as to not inhale the noxious fumes that emanated from them, but it was worth it.

It was tolerable because the word "no" never exited their lips. The Shins in Sin City had an incredible *karaoke* addiction. They were known to sing until the early hours of the morning, ordering bottle after bottle of bubbly for the girls. Afterward, they went to their respective offices, where they kept fresh suits, ready to change into, like they were the anti-Clark Kent.

When they requested Svetlana, Lula and I, we were elated, as they were perfect D.B. targets for the night. They stuttered vague compliments and talked about each other's small dick for a minute or two. Then they asked for the mikes, where they dominated the room and butchered songs for the rest of the evening.

Songs like Queen's *Bohemian Rhapsody* and the Beatles' *Twist and Shout* were accompanied by crazy, choreographed moves the Shins had invented. After every song, they looked to us for cheers and encouragement, and we did not disappoint. The more we clapped and laughed the more eager they were to choose the next song. It was quite hilarious. I watched the Shins freak out when Mikey grabbed me away and mumbled, "A-Request."

Sato-san was in his usual corner, with his delicate pale hands folded on the table in front of him. The expression in his eyes was masked by the glint from his round, gold rimmed spectacles. I was unnerved by his smile.

"Welcome back, Sato-san. How was your trip?" I had to yell because the Shins were singing so loud.

"Fine. Fine." He waved off my question in his usual fashion, not wanting to disclose anything about himself. "Let's have a *janken* contest where the winner gets a wish," he said, eager.

He was forever having tournaments of all kinds – karaoke or rock-paper-scissors, but arm wrestling was still banned because of the incident with the American girl. He loved to see the girls' competitive spirit, and whoever was luckiest on any given evening was treated to some sort of prize, whether it was money, gifts or *dohans*.

I had never been very good at rock-paper-scissors. I always lost to the snippy little scissors when I chose my rock-covering paper. We played best of ten, and I lost big time. He giggled and pretended to think about his wish.

I knew that he already pre-planned the situation, but I waited as he pouted and answered, "Let's go out to dinner at a little place I know around the corner. Do you like Italian?"

I did not want to go. I wanted to do D.B.s with the girls and the Shins. I was trying to avoid eating late at night, because I was noticing a difference in the way my clothes were fitting after the all-out calorie binges that had become my daily routine. Italian at three a.m. could not be good for my figure!

Yet in the end, Sato-san was not a person who was easy to say "no" to, so I ended up giving him a stupid, toothy grin and said, "Sure, dinner sounds nice." The matter became a zillion times worse when Ryu joined us at the restaurant soon after we were seated. It was awkward, sitting at the cramped table, looking across at both men. I tried to make it seem the presence of them together did not faze me.

Sato-san wanted me to be his flavor of the month, I supposed, with his outrageous flirting. It was obvious he was on the lookout for a new girlfriend. He was acting like a child craving candy. Ryu stared at me too, and I knew he was aware of how uncomfortable I felt. After we ate the luxurious dinner and sipped an incredible assortment of red wine, I feigned tired and yawned,

"I'm sleepy. I need sleep." My voice sounded loud and forced, even to my own ears. I hoped Sato-san would not notice anything unusual in my behavior toward Ryu.

"Can you meet me tomorrow at seven p.m. in front of your apartment?" he asked.

"Sure, of course. *Matta ne.*" I hopped into a waiting taxi. I watched out the back window as the men parted and walked away.

My phone rang and I answered an unregistered number, hoping it was my twin. She always had the power to put things straight for me. It turned out to be Ryu. It was the first time he had called me. I don't know where he got my number because I never gave it to him. And I certainly did not have his digits – not that I would call him if I did. My desire was to be pursued.

I had not expected the girls back from their D.B.s, but there was a raucous party going on in Azabu Towers when I got back that night. I was happy that curfew call was abolished, one of the first archaic rules to go. The Man tried to mask his impulse to control us by saying he was trying to protect us with the curfew. Quite simply, none of us wanted it.

Lula and Svetlana were dancing around, with music blasting, drinking champers and laughing. They stuck earplugs in the other girls' ears while they were sleeping, in hopes of not disturbing them. They kept playing *I Wanna Get High* by Cypress Hill, over and over again, which I had introduced them to that week.

They had already consumed six bottles that evening, but not with the Shins. One of the Shins had to be carried to a taxi in a drunken stupor and taken away by the time the club closed. Then the girls went "fishing," which involved scouring a room for guys that looked like Marys. They looked for red-faced, overweight men in designer suits, men who looked like they were used to getting their way.

Older geeks with bald heads and gold wedding bands were also an easy target. It was easy to strike up a conversation. The men would ask if we wanted a drink and we would say, "Oh thanks, but my girlfriends and I are just stepping into the VIP room for some *karaoke* and drinks." Then you would add as an afterthought, "You're welcome to join us, if you like..."

The night before, they fished D.B. royalty at The Crystal Lounge. Some rich Swedish dudes on business for a week in Tokyo could not wait to be shown the good clubs, no matter what the price. They did not balk at all when Svetlana asked if they could drink Dom Perignon. They did not even blink when the bill of six thousand dollars came to the table. They fought over whose plastic would cover it.

Unfortunately, the girls were not able to tip out any of the bubbly liquid. The staff in the Crystal Lounge VIP and many other D.B. establishments had strategically placed foam contraptions that you could easily tip your champagne into. That would allow you to drink more bottles and not have to be carried out drunk.

If a hostess could not get to a contraption, she could dump on the dark colored carpet. If the carpet's values had been calculated by the amount of expensive champagne that it had soaked into its synthetic fiber, it would have been deemed priceless.

The Shins just stared at the screen most of the time, so they were easy drinking companions. But for clients who required a bit more attention, it was difficult to just tip for our champagne salary.

The girls had just spent the night waiting for an opportunity to pour out champagne. Most people would think them crazy to end the evening by having to buy it anyway. Upon my arrival home, I joined them, partying until the wee hours of dawn, sipping the golden fizz and talking about the things we longed to accomplish. We watched the sun come up together and kept toasting to ourselves and to our dreams. It was ironic they seemed so much more attainable in that faraway country.

LIFE AND DEATH

"He is so buff, girls. What a body! I watched him fight last week and he knocked the other bloke senseless," Diamond gushed.

"I can't believe he's friends with Sean, Weed Jesus. Let's double date!" exclaimed Svetlana. It was hard for Svetlana to find friends to do normal things with together, especially other couples. She fingered her special cat figurine necklace with an animated smile.

Diamond had just started dating a K-1 fighter. The sport was similar to the Ultimate Fighting Challenge. It was quite brutal, but Diamond was a huge fan. She and a bunch of the other Jack's girls went to every tournament and K-1 party they could attend. I went with her to a party a week earlier, but I was less than impressed by one of the guys, who was a celebrity, a *Jujitsu* master and a complete dickhead.

I also met her new boyfriend and I could see why she was attracted to him. He was hot, but I didn't trust him. Something about the way he looked at me bothered me. Everyone's ears perked up however, because the usually quiet and reserved Sapphire had called for a meeting.

Sapphire paced the few inches that could be allowed in the tiny room and laced her white fingers together. She was wound up and so were we. We had questioned her on her strange behavior of late and we had all gotten the same evasive responses. So finally she called us over to Weed Jesus' house, crammed us into one of the bedrooms and was about to spill the beans.

Tiffany and I were late because we had taken the subway back from shopping in Harajuku. I had never been comfortable with the one line of the Skytrain in Vancouver, let alone what seemed like the millions of lines that made up the Tokyo Metro.

Thank God I had Tiffany with me. She made it look easy as she breezed around the hallways of The Tube, changing trains like it was nothing. I would have gotten lost, if not for her.

The subway had been a real trip. People were packed into cars, yet even in such close proximity they refused to acknowledge each other's existence. Everywhere I looked, passengers were sleeping, and it was still the middle of the day. They did not care if they slept standing up either. Apparently, I was the only one who found that funny. The people on the subway prided themselves on being stoic.

There were three girls waiting and lounging on the single bed together, as if on an island: Diamond, Svetlana and Lula. *Why not make it five?* I cannonballed myself into the group, high heels flying everywhere and Tiffany followed suit. No one knew that what Sapphire would share that afternoon would rock our little island and nothing would ever be the same.

Sapphire laughed a brittle laugh and said, to no one in particular, "Did you girls know that my real name is Sybil? I have always wanted to be called Sapphire, even as a little girl." She took a deep breath and confessed, "Girls, I'm pregnant."

Tiffany jumped off the bed, knocking us all together like bowling pins and screeched, wild-eyed, "Congratulations!" I had the opposite reaction and I could not disguise the look of horror that showed on my face. Lula and Svetlana overcame their shock and joined in congratulating Sapphire.

Diamond's mouth hung open for such a long time that we had to shake her back into reality. When she snapped out of it, she whispered an echo of our encouraging sentiments. "How did this happen?" she demanded a minute later, with a sense of betrayal in her voice.

"Didn't your mom have that talk with you yet about the birds and the bees?" Tiffany teased.

"Ha ha," Diamond muttered. She was in no mood to be mocked. "Takeshi and I have been using protection most of the time," Sapphire explained, "but we had slip-ups here and there. I can't take the pill because I don't want to mess with my hormones. I guess that's beside the point now." Her sentence trailed off as she looked to her friends for support. Silence pervaded the room.

"I'm about fourteen weeks now," she explained, and then she dropped the bomb. "But the really big news is that I'm getting married and we are moving up North to Takeshi's hometown, near where his family lives. We're starting a life up there together."

When Lula started crying, I thought it was because she would miss Sapphire. "It is romantic," she cried, beaming in happiness. "You will be very happy together. This is gift from God."

Sapphire in that moment looked more radiant than I had ever seen her. Even though she had already told us the news, her blue eyes sparkled at us as if she alone possessed a secret that she could never share.

I had not realized it was so serious with Takeshi. I had the sudden image of a baby with Takeshi's trademark spiky hair. It was hilarious. I laughed aloud and everyone turned to look at me, like I was about to make an important speech.

But in truth, I was terrified for Sapphire. That kind of sudden pregnancy could hinder a woman's plans. I believed we all had a responsibility to ride our wave of good fortune like surfers. But Sapphire's wave seemed more like a tsunami to me, and I was worried for her.

She was only twenty-five years old. She had no post-secondary education and could not make herself financially independent without Takeshi. She could not even speak Japanese. Yet she had decided to follow her heart. All the logical arguments did not matter in the end. Sapphire's face was shining and I knew she was excited to start her own family with the man she loved.

I remembered she told me a story about her father's alcoholic, abusive rages. Her defeated mother always turned a blind eye when he started in on her and her brother. She was deprived of a childhood and I could see she wanted to stop the cycle of abuse. "I don't have anyone in Australia," she told me with a fierce, faraway sigh. "I don't have anything to go back to."

I found my smile and said, "I think Sapphire is very courageous. We're going to have to throw you the best bachelorette party and baby shower ever!" I gave her a huge hug and rubbed her belly.

We all did, but when Diamond's turn came, she looked at her watch and said in a shaky voice, "I have to go, I have a *dohan*. I don't have time for this!"

She paused and looked Sapphire in the eyes. "You're making the biggest mistake of your life," she spat before she stormed out. We tried to console Sapphire, but she just sat there in a numb state, mumbling, "I knew that she'd take it bad, but..."

Everyone left the apartment, so it was just Weed Jesus, me and Svetlana. Svetlana sat in front of her man, looking contented with his lean arms around her. As usual, every room in Jesus' crash pad of an apartment was occupied.

The French girl and her baby had gone back to France when their visas expired. She had no intention of ever returning, as she did not make any money from her stint there. She, like every other person, had come to Japan with dreams. She wanted to open a *boulangerie* in her small province in France.

She probably could have saved enough on her own, but a hostess needed to be on call and able to move at a moment's notice. That was not an option for a single mother with no childcare. If she could not move quickly, other girls were all too ready to snap up the custie and ride his wallet for the evening.

So she left, only to be replaced two days later by some destitute Canadians. They arrived at Ana Hotel in Akasaka with only Weed Jesus' phone number, no cash and nowhere to stay. Girls did that all the time because money flowed so easily there. They thought nothing of using the last of their money to buy a ticket to Tokyo, knowing that any club would hire them in an instant.

They could probably make a D.B. on the first night back and relay their sob story to some drunken custie, who would be glad to slip them a few *ichimans*. A hostess had no reason to feel vulnerable for a lack of money. I still had not met the Canadians because Weed Jesus had taken them out for Iranian food. After that, they passed out in bed for over twenty-four hours, desperately tired.

A new, black and white bird sat in a cage next to him. I looked at it and laughed, "You are such a sucker for animals, Jesus."

He laughed like a little boy and replied, "They are my friends. They're my zoo!" Jesus really did have a thing for animals. He had two other birds, one a sad looking parrot, and a hamster named Fluffy Flavor.

He had a red-colored pit bull named Rufus. Every time I took him for walks, using his black leather studded collar, the Japanese people stared in mixed fear and envy. Our walks always elicited many shocked noises and stares. Pit bulls were rare in Japan and were a status symbol.

I was getting ready for my *dohan* that evening, in the company of my friends. I looked down at my unkempt nails with disgust, removed a nail file and started in on my right index finger with a groan. Jesus scrunched up his face in agony and cried out, "Stop!"

"He had a roommate from Israel who used to file her nails all the time," Svetlana laughed. "She had an obsession with it and she filed them down so low that they were a bloody mess. Nail filing is his pet peeve." Weed Jesus had met so many girls from so many different countries. Every girl in Roppongi knew and respected him.

"How long have you been here, Jesus?" I asked.

"It's been at least ten years, on and off. Almost a third of my life," he answered after a few minutes of deliberation. "I've had it with the lifestyle, though. It's only two weeks until we leave, Svetlana and me." They were so in love. The way that they looked at each other was so pure it lit them both up from within.

She stroked Jesus' hair and murmured, "Jesus has a really important night tonight. It's for our future. And after last night, I don't want any more tragedies."

A girl had been raped the night before. I only knew her briefly. The victim was a cute little blonde Aussie girl who had only been there a week. She went partying with the wrong people after her work at Jack's. She was given way too much coke and taken to a VIP room where she was gang raped by two men. She stumbled home and told her roommate, who immediately called Weed Jesus.

He told her that she could not go to the police about it, because she had been doing coke. The disgusting perverts who raped her might be found guilty, but so would she. In Japan, it is a criminal offense to have any drugs in your system. Jesus took charge and he called the travel agency, booking her on the next flight out of Japan and back to her family in Sydney.

Then he tried to reassure her with a promise that he would find the guys who raped her and administer his own penalty on them. "Don't worry, Amy. I will make it so they can never hurt another girl," he told her as she cried in his arms.

Whenever we girls had a problem, whether it was personal injury, fucked-up hostesses behaving badly or even overdoses, Jesus was the first person we would call. I did not blame him for wanting out. It must have been such an exhausting job, protecting everyone all the time.

I was on my way home from work, relaxing in a taxi after an evening of *dohans*, debauchery and drugs, when my phone rang. I answered Svetlana's call with a sunny, "Hi Gorgeous."

There was silence for a second. Then I heard her unforgettable, bloodcurdling wail of utter loss and heartbreak.

"Jesus is dead!" she screamed, and the line went dead.

THE AFTERMATH

Grief slinked through Roppongi like a slithering snake, winding and biting until there was not a dry female eye to be found. Clubs were shut down for the evening because the girls could not find the strength for work.

Everyone loved Jesus, many the recipients of his kindness and generosity. Stories of his chivalrous ways and deeds poured forth as everyone in Roppongi held their breath in disbelief. I don't think I could have allowed myself to believe it was true had I not been there that fateful night and seen him for myself.

When I flew in the door of Weed Jesus' apartment, I was terrified. Svetlana had stationed herself next to his bed, white-faced and was rocking back and forth on her haunches, moaning softly to herself. She looked deranged.

I never imagined coming face to face with the dead body of a close friend. I gathered my nerve and looked under the blanket Svetlana covered him with. A cold, lifeless replica of what my friend had once been lay there.

I shrank back in horror as I accidentally brushed against the body. It was stiff and hard, not at all like the warm, real man he had once been. It took all of my might to keep from losing it at that second. The only thing keeping me sane was the sight of my friend in the corner, losing her mind.

"Svetlana, listen to me. We have to get out of here!" I insisted, looking her in the eyes. She could not hear me. She was sinking, fast.

"I tried to give him mouth-to-mouth," she whimpered. Then she fell to the floor and began to scream, "No! No! No!" over and over again. Jesus' dog Rufus was sitting by her side, licking her sad face.

After much coaxing, I managed to drag Svetlana back to our apartment and got Lula out of bed to take care of her. I ran back to Jesus' house and searched it, having no idea where to find the other people who lived there or what their phone numbers were. I wanted to warn them not to come back to the apartment, but first I had to concentrate on making sure the apartment did not have any incriminating evidence lying around.

I tried to locate the piles of drugs that were a constant in the apartment, but they had mysteriously vanished. I grabbed Jesus' phone, any drug paraphernalia or personal items of Svetlana and Jesus that I found and threw them in a large, yellow plastic bag. I scrubbed the table with a warm, soapy washcloth and checked the bedroom before I ran out the door.

I stopped midstride and ran back into the kitchen, checking to see if his money stash was still in the freezer. I thought if someone had gotten the drugs, they probably had the money too. But if it had not been taken, there was an enormous wad of cash hidden inside a bag of rice. I grabbed that frozen stack of bills with one adrenaline-riddled, shaky hand and threw it in my plastic bag.

I took a last regretful look into Rufus' eyes, because I knew I could not take him with me. I was in way over my head, as it would have been conspicuous to have an enormous pit bull to explain. Everyone knew Rufus was Weed Jesus' dog. Suddenly being heat score was not as fun as it was a few weeks ago.

Meanwhile, back at the apartment, Svetlana had turned into a shrunken mute and refused to acknowledge anyone. I let her grieve as I considered our alternatives. I had cleaned out the apartment so there were no traces of us to inspire the curiosity of the police.

I knew some shady business had taken place. From what I saw of Jesus' body, it looked like he had overdosed because there was no sign of a struggle. But he was always careful to make sure he wasn't alone when he did drugs.

His death did not make sense. If someone had been with him when he died, it would have been a friend. Rufus was very protective of Jesus with strangers. It was obvious to me he had been murdered.

He was known to do hard drugs from time to time and go on binges, but he always knew when to stop. He never partied alone, and he always made sure he had a bevy of beauties who would get high with him.

He had slowed on the drugs and drinking since meeting Svetlana, relying instead on their future together. I had a feeling it wasn't an accidental overdose that had killed my friend.

I assumed he had found those rapists from the Nigerian mafia and something had gone down. But the unspoken rule we had was we never asked each other's business. I knew nothing. I did know the rapists had never been seen or heard from in Roppongi since the night of their horrendous act.

I wondered what secret business Jesus was conducting the night that he died. Svetlana told me it was a big drug deal with some big mafia boss. I thought that was weird since the mafia was territorial.

Gangsters did not deal with anyone who was not sanctioned by the mafia or a *Yakuza* group. Foreign drug dealers were in constant fear of being found out by them. If they were exposed, they inevitably faced huge fines or death.

So many people loved Jesus, but many people wished him dead as well. It would remain a mystery that would haunt me for months to come.

My best friend Svetlana became more catatonic with each passing day. She needed to get out if she was going to maintain her sanity. We told the club that one of her family members had died and she needed to go back to the Czech Republic.

We collected her wages and when she added up the cash, she had almost forty thousand dollars, including the freezer funds I found. I bought her ticket back to Prague and helped her pack. She looked so lost and weak.

When the day came to put her on the flight out of Narita, I expected her to crumble at any second. But for the first time since her partner's death, she smiled bravely and said, "This is still *our* dream."

Nothing would be the same for either of us, and we knew it as we embraced. She kissed both my cheeks and gave me a small package that I tucked into my purse as she exited through the customs doors.

I was back on the train headed for Roppongi before I opened the crinkled brown paper at one of the stops. The glint from the pewter cat figurine lit up the car with its metallic flash. A single tear slid down my cheek.

The tiny statue that had magically started my friend's love story was her parting gift. At that moment, I hoped Svetlana's figurine would start a new story for me.

NOMADICALLY ANTSY

Weeks passed and people began to forget the colorful character Jesus had been. They needed to forget. And Roppongi was a place where that was easy to do. The facade and fantasy needed to be maintained. But Roppongi would never be the same. It felt like the beginning of a beautiful demise.

My three month visa was set to expire, so I decided to go to Thailand to get away from it all. I had a huge urge to get out. It was a feeling I called *nomadically antsy*.

Christmas was coming and the last thing I wanted to do was set up a tiny tree so I would feel even lonelier in a country where the spirit of Christmas was non-existent. I was not a Christian, but I loved Christmas and still felt a rush of excitement every Christmas Eve.

That sentiment made me miss my family and want to go home. However, I knew it was not time for me to go back to Vancouver. I had work to do, although I definitely did not want to be in Tokyo for the holiday.

I thought Thailand would be as good a place as any to escape. I would just lounge on the beach and treat myself to a fancy dinner for Christmas that year. Before my much needed trip, I would have to get through the next few weeks.

I was still in awe that the world kept turning as usual and the sun kept rising after Weed Jesus' death. But I would never be the same after witnessing such a waste of a good man and friend. Everything was different for me then. I felt jaded and gypped by those tragic circumstances. I no longer had my constant companion in Svetlana and I felt so far away from my twin sister and family in Canada. I had to toughen up fast.

I wished my twin could have met me in Thailand, but she was very pregnant and did not want to fly. Part of me missed not being with her. I knew it would be detrimental to our plans to slink back to Vancouver. I would probably spend my savings in a few months and just have to keep coming back to Japan to replenish them.

I did not want to get stuck in a cycle like that, just as I did not want to be a hostess with a life sentence. My latest plan was to return from Thailand refreshed and ready to work again. The next three month stint would enable me to retire with savings of around thirty thousand dollars. That would put me in a good position to finish my CD in a nice, cozy studio and still have enough to back a small tour of the western US and Canada.

The outcome was very different from one of another of Mikey's employees, a Russian girl named Sonya, who went to jail the week before. For one entire week, the truth eluded the club staff, until one of the other girls somehow found out that Sonya was jailed for shoplifting.

She was detained at Don Quixote, a popular, seven floor extravaganza for shopping, where bargain hunters could find anything from vibrators to brand name perfume to plungers and noodles. It must have been embarrassing to be arrested at such a popular shopping place.

The panties she stole landed her in jail for a month, and then the authorities sent her back to Russia. She was deported back to Narita in handcuffs and returned to her country and family, with none of the money that she had saved.

When she was finally released, she had a month's worth of black growth from supposed platinum blonde roots, Groucho Marx style eyebrows and various hairs sprouting from her chin. The jail had a ban on tweezers and hair dye as part of their suicide safety monitoring.

I had always considered Tokyo to be a safe city. I never felt intimidated by anyone, except maybe a few forward foreigners on the twenty minute walk home from Roppongi to our apartment. Besides, I could leave my bag in a club and always expect to get it back. It was surreal how safe it seemed.

The reason most Japanese people would never commit a crime had nothing to do with the ethics of their society. It had everything to do with the severe criminal justice system, with the power to put offenders away for ridiculously long sentences. The prisons served watery *miso* soup and rotten rice twice a day. The conditions were awful and if I was a prisoner there, my only thoughts would be of escape.

After a prison sentence in Japan, it was nearly impossible to get a normal job and rejoin society. The poor people who made quick, short-sighted mistakes were deemed outcasts and were faced with no other alternative than plunging further into criminal activity upon release.

The more that I learned about Japan, the more I realized that life and society were controlled by organized crime. The *Yakuza* ran everything. They had connections in the government and in real estate. They also controlled everything that was entertainment related, from clubs to *pachinko* parlors.

Pachinko parlors were popular, smoky gaming centers that were one of the few legal forms of gambling in Japan, besides horse racing. There were monthly fees collected from all the clubs by *Yakuza* associated with certain groups' turfs for protection. Those strict fines were unavoidable.

Hiro-Depp had been employed as a manager in the illegal side of one of those gambling dens, and he told me many stories. His side job was finding "magic" *Pachinko* machines that somehow always won. He never told me how he did it, but I always imagined some sort of code breaking was involved.

All the while, I was feeling more and more alone by the day. Sapphire had gone up north to some area of Japan. I had already forgotten the name. Diamond was flying to Brazil within the week for her plastic surgery operations. She had decided to get liposuction on her thighs and tummy, too.

It was another unnecessary surgery, but I strived to be supportive. She had broken up with her K-1 fighter boyfriend, stating irreconcilable differences. I was glad she was no longer with him, because he gave me the creeps.

Lula and Tiffany were having a great time in Japan and planned on staying for as long as they could remain, but I felt a change in the atmosphere. Things were different. I was feeling claustrophobic.

So I boarded a plane for Ko Samui via Bangkok and got ready for a weeklong tropical holiday. It was my first time in a swanky hotel room and I found Thailand absolutely gorgeous. The lobby of my hotel was open air. I wore a fragrant, delicate white flower garland around my wrist that I received upon arrival.

For the first few days, my vacation included long catnaps and reading at the deserted pool. I had sensuous walks on the beach. I ate spicy Thai food and I enjoyed the roar of the ocean. I could not speak a word of Thai, so I did not speak much during my time there. I was relishing the silence. At the hostess club, you always had to be on form, entertaining someone while subtly feeding his ego. I was alone and I was comfortable with that.

Sato-san had thrown me an amazing *Sayonara* party. Like every other girl before me with a farewell to celebrate, I worked until the wee hours of the next morning. I then went partying and jumped on a limousine shuttle bus to the airport, with only a few minutes to spare. It was not a proper *Sayonara* party, as I was going to be returning in just seven short days, but I felt like I deserved a party.

I had reached my monetary goal and then some. I had saved over fifteen thousand dollars and I made another sales bonus of fifteen hundred dollars. Plus my whole trip to Thailand was funded by Sato-san. He had taken me for dinner and praised me all night before announcing in front of all the girls at the crowded table, "Here, Rose. I thought that this would come in handy," as he handed me a fat envelope with my name on it.

Curious, I opened it. The envelope contained a ticket to Ko Samui and a pamphlet displaying a stunning, exotic villa.

"I've arranged for someone to pick you up from the airport and take you to the hotel," he announced.

Of course I was happy, but I also felt manipulated because I had told Sato-san just the day before how excited I was to see my family. My flight back to Vancouver was already booked. But Sato-San knew me too well. I was happy to accept his invitation, though I had never dreamed of going to a tropical paradise like Thailand.

There was no way I would refuse that offer and he knew it. So I smiled, thanked him and kissed him on each cheek. I saw the web he was trying to spin. I saw him do it to girls before. Unfortunately however, I had no idea what to do about it.

I needed some space, so I ducked out the back door to get some air. I needed the breeze at the moment, no matter how polluted. I had no chance to consider my options because Sato-san slipped out the back door right after me.

"Oh my, Rose! Are you okay?" he said in a singsong voice, taking his glasses off. He put hands on each of my shoulders, as if to steady me, and he leaned toward me and whispered in my ear seductively, "You look so beautiful tonight."

Suddenly, rage boiled inside me for all the assumptions that customers had held in the past few months. I could not control my response. "Look Sato-san. I'm not interested," I insisted. I was not into being pursued by that powerful, aggressive man.

For the first time, his face was an open book. It first registered shock, then anger and finally settled on something in between grudging respect and dissatisfaction. He was a man who was used to getting who and what he wanted. But I also knew he was a business man who saw my value as a hostess coordinator and future money maker.

In other words, there was nothing he could do about the situation. That did not mean that I could not allow him to save face a little. "I have a boyfriend," I lied. His face lit up like a kid at Christmas, when he realized that he wasn't being rejected. It was too much for him to believe that he was anything but irresistible to women.

"Why didn't you say so?" He gripped my shoulder hard and looked at the floor as he muttered, "I need to go now, but you enjoy yourself. I'll see you when you get back."

He did not sound completely over it and as I followed him to the elevator I hoped that he could forget about the uncomfortable moment. I forgot it soon because I had so many requests the night of my *Sayonara* party. I felt like a pinball in a mad game. First Shishi, then the Shins, the Dirty Doctor and even Tokyo Gigolo graced me with their entertaining presence that evening.

Even Yazzers made an appearance. After his traumatizing run-in with Justin and Tiffany, where the term "dirty old man" destroyed his porcelain ego and forced him to run away with his tail between his legs, he had laid low. Scarred, he licked his wounds before returning to the club scene in Roppongi. And like a moth who cannot resist the flame, he was back with a vengeance for more.

The saddest part of his addiction to the hostess industry was his ignorance to the fact that the hostesses disliked him almost automatically. He had already been the custie of two of my girlfriends and they had told me identical stories.

Apparently, he would ply a girl with champagne and buy her gifts for about a month before trying to get her to go "away" with him. We knew his shelf life was about one month. So we got as much as we could before the thirty days were up. We always stayed one step ahead of him and any other such custie that thought that he could pull a fast one on a poor unsuspecting hostess.

"I want to go away to Kyoto with you," he would whine.

We saw right through to the depth of his repulsive desires as he searched without success, for a naive girl to manipulate into bed. I could think of several medieval tortures that actually sounded pleasant in comparison to being with Yazzers for more than a few hours, not to mention an entire day and night.

If you said "no," he would scout out the next recipient of his affections and subject that hostess to his inept attempts at manipulation. He always used the same tactics, and always to no avail. When the month was up and the next hostess dissuaded him again, he promptly dumped her. I did not feel bad about playing his game, because with him it was either "eat or be eaten." But that was yesterday's news.

I made a solemn promise to myself not to think about the industry while I was on vacation. There I was in a country I had never been to, enjoying myself to the fullest. I felt I deserved to wing it, knowing I created my own destiny. Nothing and no one could take that from me.

And I had such a pleasant Christmas all by myself that I was surprised! It felt good to be by myself and appreciate my own company. Over the previous three months, it was probably the first time I had ever done that. It was incredible to relish the journey and not long for the destination. Sometimes I had a hard time just existing and enjoying the life I had been offered.

I was lying on my enormous bed with a glass of champagne in my hand. Life was good. I had just gotten out of the bath and my big, fluffy white robe rode my shoulders with soft ease. I was contemplating which movie to request for pay-per-view when my phone rang.

Ring, ring, ring. The new pink phone brought me out of my reverie fast. It was the first call I had received since I had got to

Thailand. Before that, I was reveling in the luxury of not having to deal with The Man. I did not know my phone was on or that I could receive calls. I did not think that I would have reception in Thailand. Reluctantly, I answered, wishing that I had the sense to turn it off. "*Moshi Moshi*," I lisped into the phone.

"Hi Rose. Do you know who this is?" purred a deep, sexy voice. After a shocked silence on my end, a distinctly British-accented voice continued, "It's me, Edward."

Oh my God! I had a feeling Edward might call! He was an attractive, young English lawyer I had enjoyed Dom Perignon drink backs with for three nights in a row the week before. He had been in Tokyo on business and we definitely hit it off. We had not shagged, though the chemistry was thunderous. The heated energy between us left us choked up when he left, and it was not just the Dom talking.

"Hi," I croaked into the receiver.

"Let me get straight to the point. I've taken time off to see you. Are you free?" he asked.

"Kind of... I'm in Thailand right now," I answered, figuring my distant location would deter his plan.

"Brilliant. Would you mind terribly if I booked a flight? Upon my arrival, I can be your man servant," he teased in his charming fashion.

"I'm supposed to leave here tomorrow," I began. The image of Ryu's accusing face popped into my mind, but I brushed it aside, assuring myself that I was being ridiculous. We were not even dating. *You are the one who's obsessed with him, not the other way around,* I thought. *He hasn't given you any indication that he cares for you, except for one night.* I knew my decision would affect everything.

"Can't you stay in Thailand for another week, Darling?" Edward begged with enthusiasm.

With reluctant effort, I forced Ryu's face to the back of my mind. "What do I have to lose?" I replied.

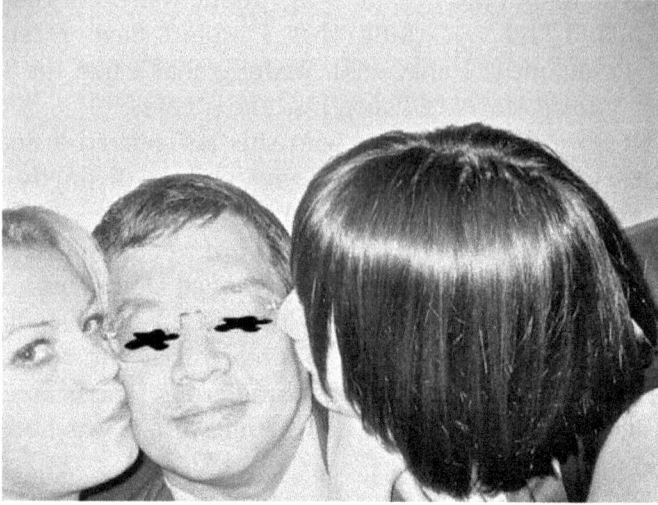

A perfect example of a happy customer

A rare shot of Shishi and his friend. He hated getting his picture
taken so much that he insisted on wearing a mask.

Another birthday at Mikey's

At the beginning of a typical night in the club

Boob Sandwich!

Halloween Party - Sitting With The Crow

Huge Hair looks so bored in the background

Karaoke party in full swing

Mikey and my beloved Aussies

Mikey's often employed sister teams - the customers loved it!

Mikey's

Mikey's before 8 and customers

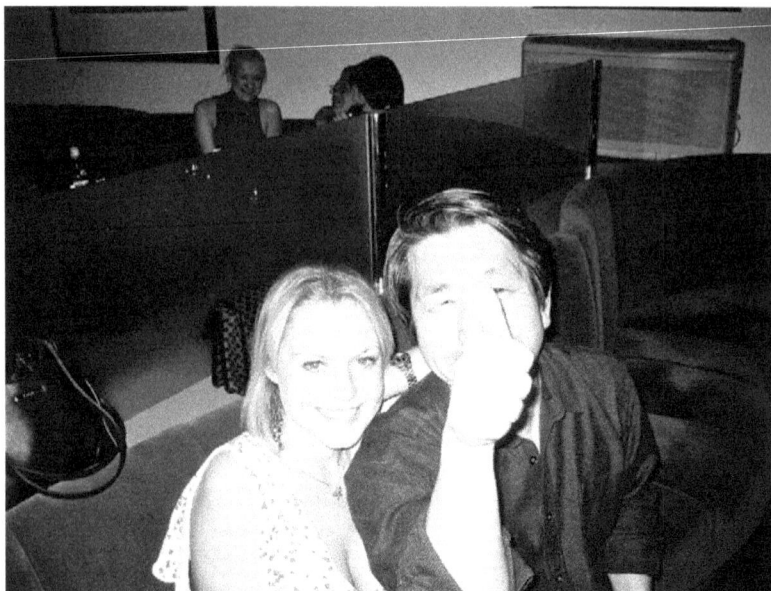

This guy was a famous customer in Roppongi. There was an ongoing debate as to whether he was entertaining or lecherous

Sato-san and a typical day in his life

The Dog Box is just starting to assemble in the background

We frequently ended up singing *karaoke* and dancing on the sofas

The night started out innocently enough...

We decided his clothes were weighing him down

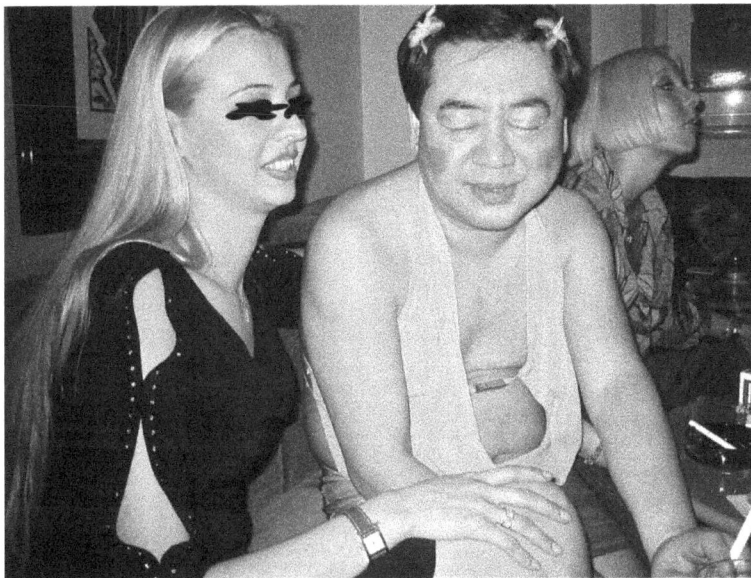

Then we put make-up on him...

After we ripped off his clothes,
we dressed him up in hostess clothes

Thankfully we had re-dressed him by the end of the night

We weren't even fazed by this customer's antics.

The hardest part of leaving a club was parting
from girls who I might never see again

The view from our apartment

TATTOOS AND INTRIGUE

The next few days seemed like pages from a romance novel. I met Edward at Ko Samui's open airport and he rushed over to scoop me up into his strong arms, calling me his angel. We decided to go to Ko Phangang Island, which boasted fabulous full moon parties, just a short boat ride away. On our way over to the island and the sunset, we were blessed with a stunning full moon. We had our first kiss under its twilight spell, awestruck by the moment.

Afterwards, we dined on the beach as the warm sand caressed our bare feet. We gazed into each other's longing eyes and fed each other succulent mangoes and pineapple. The beach was populated with small huts, lined in neat rows. From the huts came different types of music. Techno, pop and house washed over us, like the ocean waves in the distance.

I was not impressed with the music, because I would have rather been listening to some heartfelt reggae or live tunes. But as we drank Thai whiskey, mixed with Red Bull and Coke in brightly colored buckets, I could not help but go into full moon mode. I walked the beaches and saw fire limbo contests, people smoking shwaggy weed and couples getting their groove on.

The full moon party was a magical experience that I never wanted to forget, but when it did finally end, I was left in awe of it for days to come. Every morning, we walked and basked on the beach, like children, and every evening we partied and enjoyed each other's energy. The honeymoon period abruptly ended one night at dinner, though.

I had allowed myself to be lulled into a complete fantasy farce. Edward was really posh and he liked to brag about it. He was telling me all about his friend's wedding a few weeks before that was held in a castle. He had been to Eton and he was shocked I had not heard of it. It was one of the most famous schools in England, and everyone who was anyone had gone there, including Princes William and Harry.

And the night before, he made a snide comment. "There are no true Englishmen in England anymore," he sniffed. It just did not sit well with me.

When a young waiter brought over a bottle of champagne for us to try and Edward sent it back because he said it tasted "corked," I could not handle it anymore. It was more important for me to show some compassion for the poor waiter. He had been so kind and continued to be so afterward, but his eyes told me that Eddie's performance made him feel degraded and made me feel ashamed.

It was as if Edward's small mind could not see the true picture. Then I realized he was just plain spoiled. I glanced over at him, lounging on a chair with his legs crossed. He had become sunburnt while we were there, and his cheeks flamed as his brown hair tossed in the wind. It was not just the sun that had him red, though. He was still pissed off about the night before.

That night, he confronted me with a difficult question, though he pretended to be teasing. "So, how many men have you shagged?" he asked.

My first impulse was to lie and tell him a fewer number to spare his feelings. I guessed I had been with about ten guys. But after I got out of my long-term relationship, I went a little crazy with flings. I decided to tack on ten extra guys for the one night stands, which I either could not remember, or they were indiscretions my stubborn psyche still would not let me believe ever happened.

"Twenty," I sputtered. I will never forget the way his eyes popped out of his head, like a character from "Roger Rabbit." I had utterly shocked him. He tried to brush it off, but I could tell he was upset. I was not about to ask the number of people he had slept with then, since it was probably a piddley number.

He would not bring it up again, either. He wanted to forget about it and have everything surface perfect. What bugged me was his superficial kindness. He had a domineering attitude that I could not fathom, but I did not like it. There was something lacking in him, something dull about him. Worse, I was less than satisfied with his performance in bed. I found out that uptown boys don't do downtown well.

Ironically, I had been dreaming of Ryu every night. They were not pleasant dreams either. In every single one, Ryu was just smiling at me through slatted eyes, while I tried to run away or at least scream, "Leave me alone!" But my feet were heavy and I was so weak I could not move or speak. It was frustrating.

I went to Thailand to get away from the constant demands of men and there I was, shacked up with one who was growing more annoying by the day. When I tried to imagine a life that Edward and I could have together, it was terrifying. From what he had told me of his family and friends, they were all as pretentious and pedigreed as he was, with no tattoos or intrigue whatsoever.

There was no future for Edward and me. On the contrary, it was getting to the point that I could not stand the guy. I told him I was going back to Tokyo, and right away, he got weird about my work. He did not understand and I did not blame him.

With the hostess industry, men usually have to see it to believe it. They just can't understand why anyone would pay to talk. It was beyond a man's sphere of comprehension and I was not trying to explain it. In the end, he was a graceful man, as he accepted my decision.

After I packed my bags, he insisted on escorting me back to Ko Samui and to my hotel. There he pressed me with a lingering and awkward kiss. He turned, walked away and jumped into a small open aired *tuktuk*.

I only had three days left before I would return to Tokyo. I planned on spending my remaining days glued to a deck chair, taking drinks and meals poolside. I had a spectacular view when I was there earlier, so I asked the beautiful young concierge if I could have the same room. She informed me that it was occupied by my "friend."

"My friend? What do you mean?" I asked in a high-pitched voice.

She looked at me and gestured toward the couch behind me, "Your friend. He's over there."

A cold shiver of apprehension ran down my spine as I spun around. I knew who sat behind me even before I turned. It was Ryu. He was wearing a white wife beater, and for the first time, I noticed the long dragon tattoo that ran the length of his lean right arm, like a protective, fierce guardian. *How had I not noticed it when he was standing naked in my room?* I found out later the *kanji* of his name meant dragon.

He took off his sunglasses and looked me straight in the eyes. And with the same mocking, crooked smile that had been haunting my dreams for the past four nights, he replied to the concierge in broken English, "Not friend. She has friend already."

BUSTED

In absolute shock, all I could muster were the words, "What are you doing here?" I had two conflicting emotions. One came from horror that he had seen me with Edward and the other was a faint and ecstatic hope that he had journeyed here just for me.

Languid, he smiled again and sneered at me and said, "Sato-san was worried about you. Why you stay one extra week?"

"He sent you all the way to Thailand to collect that specific info?" I asked, not believing him. "He could have called."

"Something like that," he grumbled. God he was cold. I could tell he was pissed off, but I wished he had just been up front with his emotions. Instead, he was giving me half answers and his granite eyes would show me none of their truth.

It was torture. I actually *longed* for a huge fight with him. At least then I could have relieved my pent-up emotions, though I did not understand my feelings at that moment. Instead, I passed my bag to the concierge and busied myself with checking in. I needed a minute to think. When I readied myself, I took a deep breath.

"Okay, Ryu," I began, at last ready to confront the situation head on. But as he stopped me, I saw his anger recede and melt away to acceptance. He put on his sunglasses and retreated. He called out over his shoulder, not looking at me,

"We meet at lobby tonight around eight." When he said lobby, it sounded like "Robby." It was typical for Ryu to not wait for an answer and expect compliance. But I was lucky he was going to see me at all.

I was fifty percent glad he hadn't freaked out when he saw Edward. But I was equally disappointed that again, he gave me the impression that he did not give a shit about me. I was more confused than ever. It was like pulling teeth trying to get Ryu to give me a straight answer, let alone trying to get him to open up.

I allowed the bellboy to carry my bags down the winding stairway that led to the steep cliff wall. After tipping him in a handsome fashion, I donned a skimpy, black bikini and started to do a few laps in the pool. I could hear the waves crashing against the shore, adding to my melancholy mood.

Just then, I felt eyes on me and turned in the direction of the room I had occupied a few short days ago. There was Ryu, watching me. He let me see him for a few seconds before closing his curtains. Heat spread throughout the contours of my slick body as I could not concentrate on swimming any longer.

So I just lied by the pool for awhile and got up to start the "overhaul." I needed to do my nails, my hair, shave (my punani too, just in case), pluck my eyebrows and find a cute outfit that accentuated my newest accessory, a rich, deep tan. *Desperate times called for desperate measures*, I thought as I lathered my body with creams, rolled on some deodorant and applied my war paint in the form of mineral foundation, pink lip gloss, smoky eye shadow and plenty of mascara.

Earlier in the trip, I scouted out the nearest reggae bar, purchased a ripe, fat sack for about thirty dollars and sat happily smoking at poolside, on the beach and in my room for the duration of my trip.

When eight o'clock arrived, I was late and I had to call the front desk. I asked the concierge to tell Ryu I would be along shortly. Altogether, it took me almost three hours to get ready. I was still running around, curling my hair and smoking up fat doobies.

Generally a smart woman would not attempt the entire overhaul, unless she was chilling at home or she accidentally lets herself go for a bit. It happens to the best of us from time to time. The proper "overhaul" is performed in stages, because it takes a millennium to complete. But I had no choice. I needed to be in perfect working order for the talk that I would have with Ryu that night.

Once the dreaded beautification process was complete, I left my room. On the way to meet Ryu, I made a vow to myself as I climbed the steps in the pale moonlight: We were going to be together. I do not know why, but I believed it. I hoped that Ryu could forgive my encounter with Edward.

It turned out to be Ryu's first time to Thailand as well, which I thought was surprising, considering how close it was to Japan. But it was not surprising when I realized he suffered from the most common known ailment afflicting Japanese people: living as workaholics.

****

Workaholics were the reason the hostess industry existed. People worked six days a week, sixteen or more hours a day and then they were expected to go out with colleagues to a place like Mikey's to entertain that week's VIPs. Those unhappy, hastily married men comprised a huge clientele base for the hostess industry.

They sat in cubicles all day, their tired jaws hurting from smiling at people they did not like and their shoulders slumped from excessive bowing. They were similar to hostesses in the way that they always had to please others. Entertaining clients was an absolute requirement in Japan, just as marriage and children were.

"Salary Man" was a common term in Japan that described a huge majority of the population and work force. Owing to the hostess industry, those aging, overworked people had a choice to chill out and be adored hourly in the presence of a lovely lady. *What else were they going to do with their precious spare time and wads of loot?* Continuous golfing, eating and studying, the true national pastimes, began to get tiresome after a while. They needed something different and it was no shock they generally chose to unwind in a hostess environment, which was designed with them in mind.

Ryu was no exception when it came to being a workaholic. He told me about how he was at Sato-san's beck and call. He had no days off and Sato-san could call him at any hour of the day or night. I wanted to ask him what kinds of things Sato-san requested from him, but I almost did not want to know.

****

We decided to go to a great little Thai restaurant on the beach. There was a barbeque in the front, displaying all kinds of fish and seafood. We both decided on lobster and papaya salad. I sipped a pina colada and Ryu drank a frosty *Singha*, a popular Thai beer. As the evening progressed, he told me about himself, bit by bit.

"I grew up in Tokyo. I am true Tokyo boy. My papa was salary man and my mama was housewife. I had two brothers, Yuji and Shuji. Ever since I was small boy I was, different. My mother always have trouble with me, with fighting and my temper," he remembered. "I was the youngest and my *okusan* loved me best. She always stand up for me and tell me she love me." He took a shaky, pained breath and continued,

"One day, she die. I did not know she sick. Doctor say, her heart not strong enough, that is all," he said, staring at the table. You could tell he was devastated about it still. "I had nothing relationship with my father. He was not good father. All I know is that I was happy that he worked hard because he stay away. When he come home he hit me. And he hurt my mama if she try stop him. He hate me," he confided with a dark look.

"Did your father hate your brothers too?" I asked.

He paused and raised his hand, signaling to the waiter for more beer. "No. He hate me because I was not real son. My mama had lover. After she die. I had to move away. There was only me," he explained. "I had best friend. His name was Dai-chan. Him and him family was so nice to me, *always*. I was thirteen when my mama die and my friend's kind family take me in and give me kindness. Dai's father name Makoto, that meaning truth. He was first man who I really respect and look up to. I had try to find this man all my life, a father. And that man's last name is Sato."

He smiled and searched my eyes intently, for something. "Dai and me always listening to new music from America and watching movies. When we seventeen we stop school and join Dai-chan's father's group. We go to America, to Las Vegas and L.A." He stopped, and then his mood changed. "Dai-chan was killed not even two years later on his nineteenth birthday. After that, all I have is Sato-san," he anguished with a dark, brooding flash of his eyes.

"I can't even imagine what that must be like," I sympathized, "to have people so close to you die. You're only twenty-eight and you've already had such a hard time." I wondered if he had ever met his real father, but I did not ask.

"Anyway, Rose," he said, ignoring my attempt at making him feel better. "What about you? I curious."

I told him about my life on the farm and the amazing mother I had. She had been a struggling single mother of three before she met my stepdad and then my world changed. I had never experienced the kind of heartache and abuse that Ryu had, but I understood what he meant about looking for a father figure.

I only saw my biological father a couple times a year on the holidays and I felt let down by our lack of contact and closeness. He was a pretty good dad although I don't remember him being around much. In a way, my life had not really begun until my stepfather arrived, bringing with him horses, patient teachings and generosity.

Ryu listened with rapt attention. I began to feel really comfortable with him, until a few minutes after my story ended. He started the meeting.

"I have some business to talk," he intoned in an annoying fashion. "I did not want to surprise you before. First, Sato-san has left country and I go too. I leave tomorrow." He waited to see my reaction. My heart sank. I had pictured us all cozied up together on that island paradise. "Next. Police came to Mikey's and shut down," he admitted with a certain sense of defeat.

What a shock! Sato-san had led me to believe we were untouchable. I had been reassuring girls who felt raid paranoia that we had nothing to fear. How naive! It was Roppongi we were talking about. The only thing that could be counted on in Roppongi was the fact that things could not be counted on. It was a hard lesson I would continue to learn. I could not believe the impossible had happened. Mikey's had been busted!

THAILAND MAGIC

Not only had the club been busted, but Mikey and some of the hostesses went to jail. Some of my friends were sitting in prison as we spoke. My first thought was of Lula, but thank God the girl had managed to be lucky.

There was an incident and Lula was fired the night before the raid. Someone was bad mouthing one of the girls and Lula just would not put up with it. She was not one ever to start a conflict. But those at the table did not expect her fierce loyalty.

"Don't talk about her like that!" Lula demanded. Everyone stared at her in disbelief. *How dare she stand up for a friend!* Mikey bolted over and had Lula removed from the table. He was livid with her, but before he could do anything about it, Lula stood up, collected her belongings from The Dungeon and left, never to return. She would never deign to belittle herself by conversing with low class busybodies. Lula was spared because of her courage.

The Aussie girls, Kim and Karla, were released as well. They kept insisting they had been there as customers. Yes, they were dressed up in elaborate cocktail dresses, but it was irrelevant to the authorities. At the time of the bust, they were sitting with Shishi, who went down to the police station with them on his own accord. He corroborated their story.

A bunch of girls lost their freedom that night. It was tragic. They would be held in jail for thirty, long, hellish days, without even being charged. Then they would be deported back to their countries with a stamp of condemnation on their passports, denying their entry into Japan over the ensuing five years.

I was sure they prosecuted the Eastern European girls the worst, and I was right. Five went to jail, all from Eastern Europe. It turned out one poor girl had eczema and she wasn't allowed her steroid cream. Her skin broke out in boils so that by the time she was escorted home, she looked like she was in the early stage of leprosy. And worse, her family, who had expected her blinging, triumphant arrival, had to endure the shock of picking her up on the other side.

I felt lucky to have ducked out of there before the shit hit the fan. *Would I have escaped jail if I had been working at the club that night?* I did not have much faith that my freedom would not have been forfeited.

Mikey was thrown in jail because he was employing workers without proper working visas. He supposedly had an American passport. Japan was not only the country of his birth, but the country he loved. He had dual nationalities, as did many children with multicultural parents. At the age of twenty-one, he was supposed to have chosen his citizenship, whether it was to be American or Japanese.

After the arrest, Mikey had a bad name in Japan, so he chose to give up his Japanese passport and became an American national in order to get a reduced sentence. In doing so, he became nothing more than another foreigner trying to get away with illegal business in eyes of the cops.

Mikey's as a club, was destroyed on that fateful night, and I could not help being curious about how. Ryu told me the odd events that led to its demise. Mikey's had been the subject of police discussions in the days leading up to the big bust.

The club was already in hot water and under surveillance because of the Russian girl, Sonya, who was caught stealing at Don Quixote. Then Mikey's had a distraught wife of a custie complain to the police. That was rare.

Most wives were happy to get their unwanted, smelly husbands out of the house. The hostess industry was accepted with unspoken disdain, like a bad odor that could not be dispersed. To the wives, it was best left to its own devices.

But occasionally, the wife of a custie would demand an explanation about her husband's lengthy absences from the home. Some wives would become suspicious of the same old, tired excuses uncreative husbands would provide. Those wives would start to monitor the husband's phone calls, his comings and goings, etc.

That was exactly what happened to a particular custie of Susan's. Unbeknownst to him, his wife was watching him for months and had endured many nights of him coming home, smelling like booze and another woman's perfume, covered in telltale sporadic sparkles. She finally found the evidence she had been looking for in the form of a photo of said custie and Susan, just whooping it up.

Japanese women are not at all the meek creatures we have seen portrayed in the media. They are not the submissive, silent, romanticized women in kimonos they have been stereotyped to be. They are strong and they control the finances of a household and give the husband a weekly "allowance," after he hands over his pay check.

When the wife uncovered the photo of her husband lying drunk and delighted on one of Mikey's club sofas, she lost it. Susan's five-inch black stiletto heel was rammed into her husband's back, his tie lassoed around his neck, and Susan's full lips flashed a dominatrix smile at the camera.

The angry wife fumed over to the police station with her immoral pictures and let the cops have it. Shame was a powerful weapon in Japan, and she had made the police feel it. She accused Mikey of running a brothel and asked why the police weren't doing more to shut down those kinds of clubs.

Her husband would not even be questioned about it because, as a customer, he had the right to be there in the first place. But the wife's thoughts were more along the line, "If you take the bait away from the wayward fish, he won't try to bite at the dangerous line again." Word on the street was that the wife had grounded her husband for life, because he was never heard from again in Roppongi.

Well, bad news was usually counted in threes. The police already had two strikes against Mikey's when a phone call came in with more incriminating evidence pertaining to the notorious club. Sato-san was not as mighty as he had led me to believe. Yes, he worked for the *Yakuza*, the Japanese mafia, but that was a vague concept.

The Japanese mafia was not just one big gang. There were different factions that sometimes worked together or sometimes battled each other. Most disagreements were about territory. The *Yakuza* group that ran Roppongi during Mikey's heyday had changed hands. That meant that Mikey's did not have protection any longer, including protection from the police.

The mafia always had police informants to provide information. Anything from club raid schedules to other people's private information could be bought for the right price or VIP treatment. That was the reason Mikey's had always been safe. Sato-san always treated the police well and kowtowed to them. But when the new mafia group came in, they infiltrated the police and fired all police spies. Like the calm before the storm, with no warning whatsoever, Mikey's was raided.

The third strike was Sato-san. The new mafia group was pissed off at Sato-san because he owed a shitload of money to an enormous horse racing debt that he could not pay. We were all taught a valuable lesson about Japan and the world of gambling that day. Just because horse racing was legal did not mean that it was not dangerous.

So what did Sato-san do? He fled like a coward and left everybody to rot in prison. As soon as he heard about the raid, he purchased an airline ticket to a destination in Europe and left the country. He had not even paid most girls what salary they were owed. He had not visited anyone in prison or tried to get legal counsel for them. He ran away like the dog he was. I was appalled. But I was more disappointed that Ryu was going to waste his talent by joining Sato-san. I was trying to be understanding, since the man was Ryu's father figure.

Our evening was winding down, and the air between us had not been cleared. I still wanted to get to the bottom of our issues, but Ryu was acting his part of the turtle. He had already retreated to the safety of his hard shell. The night ended with an awkward walk back to the hotel and a long, lingering look into each other's eyes before we parted ways and went each to bed, alone.

I could not believe I had not summoned the courage to ask him to come back to my hotel room. I tried to get into bed, but I tossed and turned, making a frustrated, sweaty ball of my rumpled, white hotel sheets. Sleep eluded me and night continued to surround me with cool darkness, like an unwanted friend.

What I wanted was Ryu. What I needed were his hot hands on my body, their soft texture providing an outlet for my frustration. I knew I could not deny myself any longer. I did not want to resort to having sex all by myself, fantasizing about a man who was only a few meters away.

I had this life to live, and I had a responsibility to myself to go for what I wanted. *Why the constant dreams about this man? Why the constant urge to be with him?* I had to find out. I jumped out of bed, threw a fluffy white robe on over my bronzed naked body and ventured outside into the humidity, searching for Ryu. His door was only two villas down. I could see his balcony from where I stood, but the trek there seemed light-years away.

I could not deny my disappointment with him for forgiving Sato-san so easily and not empathizing more with the poor girls who waited in prison because of his boss' mistakes. I wanted to confront him about my feelings, but I knew it was not the time. I tried to push my thoughts aside as I crept over to his room and readied myself to knock on his door.

Rap, rap, rap. Here goes nothing! I thought as I knocked on his door. No one answered as I knocked again, a little louder. I was surprised when the handle turned in my hand with an easy click. *Had he intentionally left the door open?* I entered his room cautiously and searched the darkness for his sleeping body, but he was nowhere to be found.

He must have gone for a walk on the beach, I thought, but just as I turned to leave, he whispered into the velvety evening, "I waiting for you." We were to have one perfect night together before he left me with so many questions unanswered. We were to have one perfect night where we told each other our secrets.

I learned a lot about him that night. Delightful surprise number one: he had six round, silicone pellet spheres imbedded under the foreskin of the lower shaft of his dick. He was kinky through and through. It was an enormous plus on his part and he turned out to be the best lover I had ever enjoyed. Score!

Answering many of my questions about his aloof behavior, he told me he had never dated a hostess before and was wary of the occupation and those who pursued it. He had hostess issues. And who could really blame him for being apprehensive about it? He was daily in the company of hostesses and saw through all their transparent tricks and charms.

He saw through all their wheeling and dealing and ducking and diving all the way to the core of the woman. What he saw was the truth, and it was as basic as being itself. What he saw was our need to pursue our dreams.

I really admired that about him. He did not make me feel bad about being a hostess. He knew a very real and raw part of me that was too difficult to share with my most intimate loved ones, let alone a virtual stranger. He saw, knew and accepted it. I was grateful for that. I had no need to lie about what I did. Plus, I doubted that he would be able to go back to a regular lifestyle now and date a "normal" girl.

"So we definitely did not shag that first night that you stayed over in the Azabu Juban apartment, right? What were you thinking, coming back in from the shower butt naked?" I demanded.

"No, we did not sex. I just teasing," he answered with an imperceptible smile, as he played with a loose strand of my hair that lay on the pillow.

"You are a beast," I answered back at him, mocking anger. "But, I have to admit, you have guts."

"Guts?" he queried with a confused smile.

"Courage," I explained, knowing he knew that particular word.

"Why you say 'guts?'"

"Never mind. It isn't important. Next question..." I changed the subject.

"No. *My* question. Who was that guy you arrival with?" he interrupted, watching me intently. Part of me wanted to lie and answer that Edward was a friend of a girlfriend or some other lame excuse. But I valued Ryu too much to start lying then, especially when he knew so many of my bad points already and he still liked me.

"He was a boyfriend, but it's over. I won't see him again," I answered with a pleading glance. I tried to cuddle up to Ryu in the darkness, which I knew would brighten too fast. He made it clear that he needed some space, and he got up and went for a walk.

I could not sit and wait for him in angst, *but what else could I do?* When I tried to put myself in his shoes, I knew I would be jealous. Soon enough he was back. Whatever demons he had before he left were carefully concealed beneath his exotic mask of a face.

"I have good idea!" he called out to me and led me to the door and out onto the waiting, darkened shore. "Let's swim!"

PLANNING FOR SUCCESS

I did not know when I was going to see Ryu again. We made no promises to each other when he left. I finally had his elusive cell phone number, programmed in my phone, alongside the pink panda icon. What I was going to do with that information was a different question. I had to face facts. I was in love.

Did I have the balls to tell him? Of course not! I was an awkward nerd the next morning as he got ready for his flight. He told me, with an arch of his eyebrow, that he had taken one precious day off for me, but that was all he could spare.

He needed to leave as soon as possible and he seemed so serious that I did not dare question him. I didn't think it was the time, and I knew he would not give me any more information, not even the name of the country in Europe where he was meeting Sato-san.

He had to know that Sato-san and I had absolutely nothing going on, romantically. I remembered his accusing eyes the night Sato-san cornered me, and I acted on a sudden urge to reassure him, though he wasn't asking me.

"You know that Sato-san and I were just friends. There was never anything more," I tried to tell him. He did not say anything, and I could not tell whether he was relieved or not. It was not one of those goodbyes from the movies, with the passionate kiss. Ryu was shy in public and the hotel staff swarmed around us in the lobby, preparing Ryu's final departure tasks.

We hugged stiffly and avoided saying anything meaningful, but I was disappointed with my meek display. I still did not know what Ryu's motive was, working with Sato-san. *Was it just the father figure connection? Was it business related, and if so, was he in danger?* The questions kept coming. The more I knew of Sato-san, the more I worried.

I still did not know Ryu's big secret, involving his dreams. After telling him about my dreams and aspirations as a musician, I asked him much of the same. "What's your dream, Ryu?"

He had a habit of staying silent for a long time, so long that I assumed he did not hear me. So I asked once more, "What's your passion in life? What do you really love?" Again, silence. Finally, he just changed the subject.

I felt gypped. I had bared my soul the night before and told him all my dark secrets. I expected more disclosure from him so that I could begin to unlock the mystery that was Ryu.

As he lied sleeping like a baby, I wrapped Weed Jesus' male pewter cat statue in white Thai silk and slipped it into Ryu's suitcase. As I was fleeing Weed Jesus' apartment that fateful night, the tiny statue had been one of the first things I grabbed. Svetlana had insisted that I keep it and give it to the one I deemed worthy. I hoped it would protect him. We were in need of luck.

"Please let us survive this!" I prayed. Yet upon my arrival in Tokyo, I had fine-tuned the details of another of my elaborate plans. Ryu would have to be forgotten for the time being if I wanted to be successful with my plans. All he left that morning was a note on the dark wooden desk.

I expected a personal note from him, something like *I'll come back to you soon, my Darling* or some other frivolous sentiment. I'm sorry, but women want a bit of fucking romance once in a blue moon. I would not even admit it to myself at that point, but I was looking for some sort of stability or a promise from him.

But all he wrote on the stationary was, "Be good." *What a joke of a note!* But that was one of the reasons I liked him. He challenged me and did not let me take myself too seriously. I liked to be infuriated, masochist that I was. He and I both knew I was unable to "Be Good" and even less able to listen to anyone, especially when I was told to "Be Good." "Good" was a leading word, as well. It could be misconstrued.

Ring, ring, ring. I had turned my phone on less than five minutes before, but I already had a call. It was Sapphire.

"*Moshi Moshi.*"

"Surprise! How are you going? Oh…Welcome back. How was your trip?"

"It was out of this world fabulous!" I answered. "But enough about me. What about *you*? How far along are you?" I squealed into the phone.

A lady sitting a few seats in front of me in the limousine shuttle turned around and assaulted me with a foul look and a nasty sneer. Talking on the phone was frowned upon in the limousine shuttle. I tried to keep it down.

"I am six months along now, and I am getting enormous," Sapphire laughed, speaking a mile a minute. "At the end of my Roppongi stint, I was getting sick of trying to hide it behind baggy, black shirts and trying to cover up my lack of alcohol consumption. Takeshi has taken a job with his dad," she continued. "So he's gone most of the time. I hang out with Takeshi's mom, but she doesn't speak a word of English. She is so sweet, though and I am trying my best to learn Japanese."

I could tell that Sapphire was content. I had never heard her sound so bubbly and full of life.

"How's being pregnant?" I asked as I wrapped the white *pashmina* around my neck, reacting to the air conditioner.

"Oh you know, all the usual lovely symptoms. Constant peeing, my ankles are nonexistent, aches and pains everywhere. I can't even keep my fitness up by going to the gym. Just going for a walk tires me out," she complained.

"What does it feel like when the baby kicks?" I had no idea what it was like.

"It's supposed to feel like butterflies, but it feels more like a clawing sensation. Anyway look, I am coming to Tokyo next weekend. Even though a girl is pregnant, it does not mean she can't party a bit and go out with the girls. I'm getting bored here and I need to get out. Even Takeshi thinks it would do me some good," she explained.

"Coooool! Well you can definitely stay with me. I would be happy to give up my bed for a preggo," I laughed.

"Ha ha. *Too* funny! Thanks, Rose. You are a doll! See you next weekend. Kisses!" and she hung up.

"Bye, Sweetie!" I was elated at the thought of seeing her again so soon. I didn't bother telling her any of the news involving the bust at Mikey's. In fact, I did not even have a bed or an apartment to offer her. I had to get my stuff out of the club apartment as soon as possible because my room there would soon be rented by the new tenants. I didn't want to stress Sapphire out in her delicate condition.

Besides, I had called Pin, the notorious Roppongi slumlord. I would secure one of his filthy dives. I called Tiffany. After about twenty rings, she finally answered the phone in her gravelly voice, "You're back, Savage! I'm assuming you've heard about Mikey's. It's shocking, isn't it?"

"*More* than shocking! Look I'm on the shuttle bus coming back from Narita. Can you do me a favor and let me crash at your place tonight?"

"Of course, Darling," she answered. "I'll see you here soon. Lula's staying at my place too, so it'll be quite the hen party. I'll put the kettle on. *Ciao*." When I got to her apartment, I had an overwhelming urge to get into some comfy clothes. Lula was sleeping soundly on the couch. I felt pleased that she was okay.

"I gotta take off these pants. They are chafing!" I exclaimed. Tiffany looked at me with an alarmed expression before her face relaxed into a smile,

"Oh? You mean *trousers*! What you call underwear, we call pants in the Queen's English," she giggled. I laughed at her posh accent.

"Stop taking the piss. I should give you some proper English lessons," she quipped back.

Tiffany, the world's best hostess, had run me a hot bath. As I submerged my aching body in the scented waters, I reveled in the fact that I had such good friends. When I exited the bath an hour later, Tiffany had a glass of champers waiting for me, and we toasted, "To success!" I clinked my glass against hers and she looked at me.

She had no idea what I was talking about, but she was used to my crazy plans. I did not know it at the time, but that fateful toast would bring us real wealth. The question was, "Did we really want it?"

GFE

I remained still behind the two-way mirror with four other girlfriends, not breathing and staring in horror at one another. When the police rushed into the room, the cabaret show ended like the slowing down of a record machine. They were looking for us. They went about questioning people and checking ID cards, while we waited only a few meters away, watching them.

The popo finally left and we came out of hiding, acting like nothing even happened. The police questioned girls in the club, but they all had legitimate visas, mostly obtained from marriages to Japanese man. As for me, my whole reality changed in the blink of an eye, again.

For starters, I had gone to work at Jack's, the most famous club in all of Roppongi, with over one hundred hostesses employed there. There was a Japanese hostess side of the club. It was a larger space with three cabaret shows a night and a connected strip club next door, called "Private Eyes."

At Jack's, custies could find a variety of entertainment. It was a one stop shop. I worked in the main area, with at least fifty to seventy different girls, from all over the West. No one had *Sayonara* parties at the club because there were too many of us to keep track of which girls were coming or going.

Another aspect that differed Jack's from Mikey's and other clubs was the lack of *karaoke*. Instead of custies sitting around, wailing out well-known tunes, there was top forty and hip-hop music blaring from the enormous black speakers positioned at the back of the stage.

The cabaret show was nicely done and only semi-nude. I liked the break from speaking with custies, as it gave me much needed time to think and plan. The sexy girls twisted and gyrated in rhythm to choreographed dances. However, the VIP entertainment was not well presented from the customers' perspective. Guests did not have a good view of the stage and the cabaret show.

Many famous people frequented Jack's. The men and women who came would usually be seated in the VIP area. As a rule of thumb, most VIPs liked to be seen pretending they were trying not to be seen. Most were Japanese politicians, rich businessmen and an occasional Japanese celebrity. I never had any clue who those celebrities were, but some were good tippers.

I really liked working at Jack's because I could wear what I wanted. With all the police crack downs, girls were told more and more to dress "normally," so the police would believe they were customers in the event of a raid. Employers were not trying as much to protect the girls as they were at protecting themselves. If they were caught employing girls without proper visas, they could get a huge fine, or get closed down.

The dresses we had been forced to wear at Mikey's created a role relationship between the hostess and the customer, allowing guests to forget we were real people. Being able to wear what we wanted at Jack's put us on more equal ground and empowered us.

It also intimidated customers less. I actually wore a track suit and running shoes to work one day, a damn cute one of course! I got a great response. It was something different and many customers just wanted to talk to a real girl, not a hostess.

I already had a crew that consisted of Tiffany, Lula, Amy and Crystale, the two impoverished Canadians that Weed Jesus rescued. I was hiding with those four girls that night. One of the waiters ran up and warned us, whispering, "Hide behind the two-way mirror!"

On the day we started work at Jack's, management briefed us on what we were to do during a police raid, but that night was our first time implementing it. We had to put our glasses down and tell our custies, "I'll be right back," before slipping unnoticed behind the mirror.

Our time at the club continued to fly by as we learned that and other valuable lessons. There was more to being a hostess than tipping out our drinks to up our bill. We learned to order "Lady Specials," better known in our circle as an LS, which was a twenty dollar glass of club soda that custies paid for, thinking it was an alcoholic drink.

But sometimes a custie who had been around the block was wise to the LS. Tokyo Gigolo was one of those custies. He howled when I tried to order one and said, "I no pay for soda. Just for that, we drink bottle of tequila."

We had to take care with those custies because they knew trade secrets. As hostesses, we had our own rules. One was "no talking about another girl's boyfriend at a table." That was unheard of behavior. Another no-no was telling custies about D.B.s, LSs and other confidential hostess business. Doing so would ruin custies for the next girl. It was better to let a custie believe he had taken a girl for a ride.

But some girls blabbed, and the result was a custie who reached full maturity long before his time was up. Thank God I did not have any custies, besides TG, who were so used and jaded.

****

As expected, I found an apartment through the lecherous Pin. I was glad for the connection, and I didn't even flinch when I saw the atrocious state of the unit he tried to show me. I began to clean the apartment from top to bottom. I threw my used cleaning clothes and all the rags into the trash after I was done, like the toxic waste it was.

After having a hot shower in the cramped bathroom, I jogged up to Don Quixote and bought items for my new pad. Pin supplied me with a futon, TV, small table, miniature fridge and some kitchen stuff. So I bought new bed linens and blankets, a nice, fluffy pillow, a full length mirror, an extra futon for guests and a DVD player.

I was set up, but I could not help but curse Pin when the taxi dropped me off with my huge, yellow shopping bags. I remembered then that I lived on the *fifth* floor, with no elevator! At least I would be getting my exercise by climbing those stairs every night.

I turned on the TV and found there were no English channels. I flipped through the bizarre stations that made up Japanese television, my eyes crossing as I watched weird talk shows with people behaving in insane ways.

I sat back and rolled a toothpick-sized doobie and enjoyed every last puff. That joint had cost me close to fifty dollars. I figured if there were ten good pulls in the dube, then each puff had cost me about five bucks. But it was worth every yen.

I was researching where to get weed, but everyone had the same connection, Weed Jesus. I was forced to hit the streets and ask some dodgy looking Nigerian guys if they knew where to get some. None of them did. They had copious amounts of coke and crystal meth, which was the drug of choice for most in Roppongi. It was less stinky and easier to transport.

Many girls at Jack's used one or the other, but I was not interested in that shit. I vowed to stop snorting that filthy, addictive coke. I had already watched girls I knew turn into skeletons and shells of their former selves, the result of consuming too much of the white powder.

The dodgy dudes were finally able to hook me up with Tony, a short, gapped toothed Nigerian with a huge smile, who worked at the local reggae bar. I called him Ganja Tony. I was grateful for the smoke, no matter how leafy and overpriced it was.

Later that day, I stomped down my new ghetto apartment's stairs because I decided to go shopping for Sapphire's baby. It was frustrating shopping for a baby when I did not know what sex it was.

I was tempted to buy the pink, frilly girly things, but in the end, I decided on a neutral, green baby outfit and a matching polka dot hat. Her half Japanese baby was bound to be adorable and I could not wait to see him/her in the tiny getup.

I waited for her at the designated spot, the ANA Intercontinental Hotel, and readied myself for my burgeoning friend. I was excited to see her.

 She was radiant when she got off the bus, radiant and huge. She had on a black cloaked jacket and wore dark Chanel shades. Her glamorous fashion, along with platinum blonde hair made her stand out. I was certain she drew questioning stares from her new neighbors in rural Japan, where foreigners were uncommon, let alone a Marilyn Monroe reincarnate.

She dashed over to me at full speed. *God, she could move fast for a pregnant woman!* Then she checked herself and slowed her pace with a chuckle, "My doctor told me to slow down a bit," she confessed.

"Ya, I guess so," I answered and opened my arms for a hug. "You look great!" She hugged me against her expanding belly and stepped back to do a little twirl for me. She definitely had a bump, and it was cute. Then I saw a familiar face as a shock of perfect raven hair flashed toward me.

Sapphire laughed with delight, almost singing, "I have a surprise for you!" It was Diamond! She looked spectacular as well. Her curves had always been lovely, but the way she filled her thin white trench coat post-op was *va-va-voom!* I could see the results myself.

"Oh my God, Rose! It's so good to *see* you! Aww! You look gorgeous! After Brazil and the surgery," Diamond explained," I went back home to Sydney for a few months, but I'm back now. I'm almost at one hundred percent. I had some pain in the first few weeks, but it's all good now. How are you?" She was still the same sparkly, endearing creature she had always been.

As we stood there, an attractive lady with a black teacup poodle walked by. The dog was wearing a matching red, feathered hat and red leather jacket. It was identical to the one worn by its master. They made quite the pair. We could not help but stare as we all burst out laughing. The woman smiled and continued on her way, displaying her adorable dog like an award.

"Only in Japan!" laughed Diamond. "I'm experiencing definite culture shock at the moment."

"So, how's the custie situation for you at the moment, Rose?" Diamond asked. She was obviously planning another stint, as she needed to get the lay of the land.

"All my custies from Mikey's came to see me at Jack's after the bust," I answered. "Shishi, the Shins, TG, The Crow, Yazzers, the works."

I had only worked at Jack's for a week until then, but I was seated with umpteen custies a night. I also created a whole new crew of customers as well. I did not know it then, but I had hit my peak popularity as a hostess. I was the flavor of the month and everybody wanted a taste!

Custies were flocking. There was plenty to be had. I thought I would not get as many because there was no *karaoke*. I got numerous custies at Mikey's because of my love of *karaoke*.

"But at Jack's I have just been targeting the most Mary customer I could find in any given evening," I admitted. "Eventually, I would ask him if he wanted to go to *karaoke* after the club. I usually took him right next door to Crystal Lounge and did drink backs there. Nano, the manager, knows us and gives us great service. We had eight bottles last night, between Lula and me. That night we each made about eight hundred dollars just in D.B.s, plus our salary, which was two hundred fifty dollars. Oh ya, and we got five hundred yen per drink to a maximum of twenty-five drinks per night, for one hundred twenty-five dollars extra. I made almost twelve hundred dollars last night for doing shit."

If we saved our money and continued to have such profitable nights, we could build a nest egg. I had already saved fifteen thousand dollars after all my expenses, but I decided to set my goals a little higher. My new aim was to add another thirty-five thousand dollars, equaling a tidy little sum of fifty thousand dollars in savings. I thought the goal was doable.

Diamond's eyes lit up when I told her how well we were doing. "Good! Cuz I'm skint after all the surgeries and traveling," she laughed.

The last time I saw her she was really pissed off about Sapphire's pregnancy. But she had a complete change of heart when faced with the possibility of losing her best friend. So Diamond begged Sapphire's forgiveness and showed her gratitude by coming all the way out to the boonies of Japan and spending the last couple weeks hanging out with pregnant, bored Sapphire and her elderly, Japanese mother-in-law.

Another surprise was that it was Sapphire's birthday. I wished she had given me some notice, though. "Happy Birthday!" I exclaimed when they told me. Then I started thinking aloud, "I wish it was my birthday. Then I would have an excuse to get lots of presents from customers!" I laughed.

"Oh, but it *is* your birthday, Darling," Diamond stated, matter-of-factly.

"No, it isn't, Diamond," I replied.

"The *custies* don't know that," she quipped.

"Yeah! You could have a fake birthday!" Sapphire chimed in.

"That actually doesn't sound like a bad idea," I answered after a moment. I would put that plan on the back burner until later.

"But seriously, what do you want for your birthday?" I inquired.

"I've been telling Diamond what I want the whole way down here. I want details," Sapphire giggled.

"What *kind* of details?" I asked as I glanced over at Diamond's blushing face.

"Oh, all right. I shagged a monk, okay," Diamond whispered with a devilish smile.

Sapphire let out a high-pitched squeal and collapsed into hysterics, "I knew it. I *knew* it!"

"But in my defense, he was a wicked monk," Diamond retorted, trying to make our laughter subside.

As it turned out, Takeshi had a buddy who was a monk. His whole monk family lived in houses right on the temple grounds. Being a monk in Japan seemed quite the profitable occupation because this particular hunky monky was loaded and drove a really nice car.

Back in the old days, they were forbidden to eat meat, have money or even to have sex. But things had changed. Diamond's monk was a reggae music DJ, he could speak English and best of all, he ate meat, as well as pussy, with the best of them.

"That's a pretty big change, from a K-1 fighter to a monk," I joshed.

"Well, what can I say?" she shrugged. "I'm a changed woman. By the way, I wanted to ask you a favor. Can I stay with you for a bit?"

"Of course. I was meaning to offer. Lula might move in too, though. We can crowd in. We're used to it," I answered.

"Sweet, thanks for that! How is your twin anyway?" she asked in her cute Aussie accent.

"Actually, I have been keeping her busy during her pregnancy. She's a Canadian hostess recruiting agent," I explained. "She put an ad in the newspaper, takes girls' info and photos and sends them to different clubs to be considered for work. She gets eight hundred dollars per girl. She's about to pop out her baby any day now, though. I'm excited!"

Sapphire looked uneasy with the "pop" terminology and vulgar hand gestures that I used to mime birth. By the time we stopped talking and listening to 2Pac, we were beat. So we lined up futons in the tiny apartment to prepare for our slumber party. We all laughed at the sight, as the futons took up the entire floor space of the apartment.

"This whole apartment is the size of my bedroom back home," Sapphire sighed, marveling.

"Space is overrated," Diamond commented with a grin.

Like little kids, we all jumped into what seemed like one big bed and said our "goodnights" to each other. We tried to shut our eyes to close out the excitement around us and get some rest.

The next morning came sooner than I had anticipated. I cursed myself because I had to meet a customer a couple hours later for dinner.

Meeting Tom was uneventful. His unremarkable face swam before my eyes in a sea of unmemorable faces and meetings. I had probably met at least fifty different guys that night. So I did not remember him when he came into Jack's the following night to request me, but I greeted him with confidence and a practiced smile, as I purred, "Great to see you again." He looked delighted I had "remembered" him.

Meanwhile, I was sitting with my new best buddy, The Crow. He had been coming in to see me almost every night. We hadn't really talked before at Mikey's, with his horrendous *karaoke* addiction and my own willingness to turn a blind eye to it. I repeatedly offered him his drug of choice, the microphone.

But now it was The Crow and me, one on one, with no *karaoke* buffer. I knew everything about him and it was starting to affect me outside the workplace. I thought of him often because I felt bad for him. I was starting to feel protective of him, and that was a professional no-no.

The truth was his life sucked. Like every other custie I knew, he was in a loveless marriage. I never understood why they just wouldn't get a divorce. They just don't. It was unheard of. Supposedly, his wife could not stand him and vice versa.

Most of those young marriages were a waste. Who knew what journeys were possible, given freedom in those tumultuous early years. It seemed they were robbed of the experience of finding themselves and defining their identity.

I tried to imagine my divorced parents still together and could not. They were just unsuitable as a couple. It is too bad that freedom of expression was not stressed more in that generation of

Japanese people. They had the chance at passion and magic stolen from them. The main reason that a customer walked through the door of a hostess club was for the pursuit of those intangible desires.

The Crow was so physically repulsive. I could not imagine what that would be like. Our world views physical beauty as essential and precious. Our status was based on outward appearance and I sometimes forgot how lucky I was to have been born possessing a popular idea of beauty.

He worked like a dog for a company at a job he despised. They devalued him. He was just another number, another salary man. As a boy, he always listened to American rock and roll and even dared to dream that he might one day travel to that faraway land. But alas, he had never traveled outside Japan and it haunted him.

He dwelled on suicide more than what was normal in a country whose suicide rate was among the highest in the world. He was depressed. As he started to open up to me more and more, I became affected.

For the two weeks leading until then, I saw him *every day*. That meant his life consisted of three main elements, work, clubbing and sleeping. He never saw his family, and when he did, he often started arguing with his wife.

Yet every time I saw him, he would pull out his two tattered and outdated wallet photos of his twin boys and show them to me, wistfully. It was as if he needed my energy. It was the first time I started to actually care about a customer, instead of seeking to use him for his money.

In a way, a customer and a hostess were similar. They needed each other to survive, and both wanted the other to view them as if they were just a normal person. The Crow was no different.

I felt his desperation when I was removed from the table to sit with another one of my custies. I was his lifeline to a kind of sanity and reality he needed. I did not know how to help him, so I just kept silent and listened to his pain. Later that night, I was still thinking about The Crow, but I willed myself to snap out of it and get my game together.

Tom and I ended up at *karaoke*. He came on a *dohan* with me and waited patiently all night as I was moved from table to table. Even if a custie requested a girl, it did not mean that he got to sit with her all night. I had other requests and customers. Even though he had to wake up at six the next morning for a golf tee time, he stayed out with me until five and drove to the golf club reeking of booze.

He asked me the inevitable question, "Do you have a boyfriend?" He was not looking at me, trying to make his question subtle.

"Yes," I replied as I watched his face drop.

"*You!*" I whispered.

He beamed at me with a huge, yellow-toothed smile and clapped his hands together in delight. I had answered correctly because he was the definition of a generous Mary. When I asked for champagne, he waved his hand dismissively and answered, "Anything you want."

I liked that answer, so I was on my best behavior all evening, giving him my unfailing attention. I could already see what he wanted and needed, a GFE, a girlfriend experience. He was so mesmerized by me already that he would have been happy with a fake GFE. All that would have involved was me listening to his stories about work and sympathizing while seated with him at a romantic restaurant. I learned to ignore onlookers who tried to guess whether or not we were involved.

Was he a sugar daddy? No, because the term "sugar daddy" was attached to sex, and I certainly would not be shagging him. A GFE had nothing to do with sex. I knew Tom would never have the balls to have brought it up either. I heard horror stories about custies pulling up in front of love hotels and demanding the girl go with him or he would never come to the club to request her again.

I never experienced that kind of perverted customer and I was positive Tom was not one of them. He was just a rich, bored older guy who needed some cute girl to spend money on in return for a little TLC and a little GFE. It was another stroke of luck to have met him, because he turned out to be the most profitable customer of all time!

HAPPY FAKE BIRTHDAY!

My five fellow roomies were crammed into a space that was not big enough for even a half person, let alone a brigade of hostesses. I looked over at my friends sleeping and chuckled at the sight of them. To my left, Lula was cuddled up to me, snoring softly. Her eyes were hidden behind an oversized sleeping mask. To my right, the destitute Canadians, Amy and Crystale, lay zonked out, oblivious to the world.

Diamond lied at our feet, makeup still intact, except for a fake eyelash smashed into the side of her face. She slept on a yoga mat with someone's jacket thrown on for a blanket. She was the last to come home that morning and was forced to opt for the least attractive sleeping arrangement.

I was surprised earlier that week when I was moved from a table and led to another one, where two glamorously dressed women sat. One was a tall brunette and the other a petite, pretty girl who looked Latin. I had no idea they were Amy and Crystale.

They came into Jack's, seeking employment, and were hired on the spot, just like me. Their story differed from mine. They came across bad fortune. The night Weed Jesus died, they were out partying all night and stayed at another friend's house. When word reached them of his death, they steered clear of the apartment, abandoning all their stuff in the process. At least they were spared having to deal with police questions.

They were not in town long before the tragedy. They worked their sad story on an unsuspecting custie, who moved them into his gorgeous spare apartment for a few weeks, but after Weed Jesus died, they were homeless again.

Someone told them about Pin's slums and they moved into a new abode, which was an apartment building that housed hostesses, strippers and other Roppongi workers. The club they were working in was along the same idea as Mikey's, but it was in Ginza.

Like me, it was their second hostess stint, but they felt comfortable working a familiar club. They did not know how great it was to work at Jack's. Their club had the old controlling rules with an older Japanese *mamma-san* who made their lives miserable. She was always trying to stiff them.

Ginza was supposed to be a high class area, but I could have cared less. The clubs in that area were an absolute nightmare. First, most custies did not speak a word of English except for the phrase, "I do not speak English." Ginza boasted a different class of clients, who were a lot more conservative.

The second atrocity at the Ginza club was that everyone in the Dog Box had to stand up, smile stupidly and say *Irashaimase!* when a customer walked through the door. It was so demeaning! Most of the time, custies did not even acknowledge the effort.

The third and most demeaning task the job demanded was some tacky hostess parade. A cheesy manager would introduce the girls to the club's customers. For example, he would announce, "Here's Amy from Canada!" At that point, embarrassed, the girl had to get up from the table she was sitting at and prance around like a skank, doing her imitation of a model walk. It was just sad. Girls dreaded it more than a Brazilian bikini wax!

To make matters worse, there were two annoying *skebbae* hostesses working at that particular club. One of them was an English girl who would literally get up on top of her customers and pretend to ride them while making moaning noises into the microphone. She was shagging all her custies, even the foulest of the foul. It made all the other hostesses look bad. We did not want our customers to expect the same treatment.

Normal hostesses tried to chat and have conversations, all the while trying to figure out how to get out of "cheek dancing" with custies. But when that *skebbae* hostess got going, everyone stopped to look on in shock and horror as that chick went insane.

She was happy to have a place where it was acceptable to act out her sick fantasies with an audience. She wasn't all there. The funny, but unsurprising fact: *she was the number one girl in the club!* I guess there were many sick custies out there as well. You attract what you put out. The staff loved her, too. I kept expecting the management to ask her to tone it down, but they just egged her on.

The second *skebbae* hostess was a Russian girl named Anna, which means "hole" in Japanese, with a terrible alcohol problem. She was a stunning blonde, who was actually harmless without hooch. But early every evening, she started drinking straight, hard alcohol. If someone tried to take the booze away from her, she would find the first available table, grab the bottle off it and start swigging.

Drunk, she would start her nightly unscheduled "show time." It would be an erotic, disjointed dance that was so *all over the place*. She often fell over. She was never embarrassed though, as she picked herself up from the sticky carpet and continued running from table to table, shocking the startled though curious custies.

Many thoughts ran through my head as I watched those girls. For me, a multitude of the world problems could be illustrated just watching those hostesses. A person could easily judge them or find them disgusting or even want to take advantage of them.

But mostly I felt pity for those girls. On the surface, Anna's show times were so out there they were comical. However, if you allowed your brain to think that way, you would miss out on the bigger picture. The girls were running from something. It must have been something scary too, because they would do anything to run as far away from it as they could get. They stopped loving themselves a long time before, and some sort of abuse or mental illness must have caused it. It was sad.

Anyhow, I preferred the *skebbae* hostesses to the fake ones, because at least the former provided a sense of entertainment. The fake hostesses were plain boring. Those bitches would stare adoringly at some Mary *all* evening.

They engaged themselves in an abnormal gazing battle, which was almost always followed up with a rave about how great the custie was. It was blatant brownnosing. I could not stand it, but it was really common in Ginza clubs. A fake hostess was not there to make friends, but to get custies, whatever the stakes.

It was clear to me that Amy and Crystale had never belonged in Ginza. They belonged in Roppongi. For that reason, their luck was bad and got worse each day. They finally got their monthly wages from their Ginza club and quit on the spot, so they could start working at Jack's. They stuck their wages in their underwear drawers, each withdrawing an *ichiman* from their "banks" to take themselves for a nice dinner to celebrate.

That very night, they were robbed. Every last yen was taken, all their savings. Someone had targeted them because the apartments were known to house hostesses and probably contained money. So they were homeless again. They did not have enough money to pay the next month's rent. Even if they did, they would not have because they felt unsafe after arriving home to a drilled through door.

It was a good thing they had jobs at Jack's in Roppongi, where the streets were paved with yen, and hostesses could roam freely from table to table, being fabulous. On a whim, they asked the manager if there was a Canadian hostess named Rose working there. They were surprised when I came over to meet them.

Apparently, they remembered Weed Jesus' stories about me. He told them we should get together and that we would all get along. That was another way Jesus touched us all, even from beyond this earth.

After they explained their sad situation to me, I asked them if they needed a place to stay. I drew them a small map that pinpointed the location of my apartment and gave them my keys, asking them to leave them in the mailbox if they wanted to go out.

They both looked gorgeous. The tall girl, Crystale, was sporting a slinky, white silk, one shouldered mini dress. She complemented the sexy number with funky, sparkly earrings that hung almost to her shoulders alongside her sleek, brown bob.

Amy, a petite girl, had a shock of unruly, dark hair, which complemented her olive complexion and baby face. She wore a more conservative, grey wool dress that seemed demure until she turned to grab her black, patent leather Salvatore Ferragamo evening bag. I caught sight of her bare back and I realized that the dress was far more stylish than I initially thought.

But no matter how gorgeous they looked, I could see through their masks. Underneath all the glitz and glamour, the sparkles and jewels, they were exhausted. They made a hasty exit to my apartment to hit the hay for a good two-day hibernation session. After resting, they became themselves again. They had been through so much.

So there we were, all of us living in one small room and making the best of it. We laughed as we continuously bumped into each other. Our apartment's art consisted of a myriad of suitcases and cosmetics. We learned to take lightning fast showers in order to accommodate our ever growing hostess brood. I took on the task of *mamma-san* again and I felt at home with it.

I got up and started making breakfast. The kitchen consisted of a tiny sink and one burner, side by side. The only other appliances were a pint-sized fridge and a burnt out microwave, sitting precariously on top of it.

Lula did not have to be there. She had saved enough money to get her own ghetto Pin pad. The reason she decided to stay in such cramped quarters was her strong fear of being alone.

I observed it in the first days that we met, but I was convinced it would subside as her confidence grew. But until then, her fears had not gone away. On the contrary, they were even more apparent. She would rather stay out all night with me than walk home by herself after work ended.

I was happy with the arrangements too. In Canada, I always had my sister to hang out with, while sharing my innermost secrets and desires. I found my pseudo twin in Svetlana, and I had an amazing crew of girls.

Even though I was surrounded by beautiful friends, I could not help feeling lonely and unfulfilled. I loved my twin in a way that few people will ever know. I knew I was lucky to experience such a powerful emotion, but with that gift came great pain as well. I was trying to keep myself busy to avoid thinking of my sister. The last time I saw her was not a pleasant memory.

Barbie had not lured just *me* in with her seductive stories of Japan. My sister, Daisy, was equally smitten. Daisy and I were planning to take Japan by storm, double-trouble style. But one night, she sat me down and told me I would have to fly solo to Japan, because she was pregnant. What was worse, her boyfriend at the time was questioning his sexuality and needed his distance. They ended up calling it quits a few weeks later.

Our dreams to travel and write music together died before my eyes. I was verbally abusive and uncaring to her that night, and it haunted me still. I acted out in a similar fashion to Diamond, when she found out about Sapphire's pregnancy. That was the last time I saw my twin, and I could not help but imagine my vibrant, pregnant young sister, struggling to make ends meet by working two jobs.

Of course, I spoke to her on the phone and sent money to help out. We had patched things up between us. But I was still beating myself up and I still felt ashamed about my behavior. I was forced to accept that life does not work out the way people plan, most of the time.

I refused to give up my faith that destiny would always have meaning. Our mother taught us "The Mother" would provide and that our role in life was to be as compassionate and loving as we could be. I needed to keep striving for that.

My negative energy stemmed from feeling unfulfilled in my music. The effort I put into calling and going out with customers left me drained of my creativity. I had not written music in so long that I began to dislike myself. I was using booze, coke and weed to forget that.

The afternoon light streaked through a cloud, directly into my eyes, reminding me to wake the girls so we could begin our day. We needed to rise and shine around the same time in order to maneuver around the tiny apartment.

The best way to do that was frying up bacon. Even the strictest vegetarians in our household could not resist the smell of the Canadian back bacon I bought from Nissin, the overpriced International supermarket. It was an extravagance I could not do without.

Just as I was about to hurdle bodies to get to the teensy, battered gray fridge, my phone rang. I already knew, without looking, that it was The Crow. He had come in to see me almost every night, even though Jack's did not possess any *karaoke* machines. At first, I was stoked, because I really enjoyed his company and his sweet demeanor. But after we lost the camouflage of *karaoke*, I began dreading his visits to the club. I felt like his psychiatrist. He was so unhappy.

That same urge to shelter him came over me as I listened to his sad stories. It was ironic that his dream was to be an international rock star, and yet he had never traveled outside Japan.

I picked up the cold phone and was not surprised when the flashing words on my phone read, The Crow. "*Moshi Moshi,*" I spoke, trying to sound energetic.

"I can't come tonight. I had a happen last night! A big happen!" The Crow shrilled into the receiver.

I moved the receiver far away from my head and asked with a sympathetic tone, "What kind of happen?"

"I lost much money! Too much money!" he shrieked even louder.

"Calm down. Everything will be all right." He was such a drama queen. He was forever calling me with the latest about his crazy, incident filled life.

"I drunk over last night. I was, with friend." He was always thinking I would get jealous if he went to another hostess club.

"Don't worry. I know where you were last night," I reassured him. He was a terrible liar, and I knew for a fact that he had been at a strip club in Roppongi the night before.

My Aussie girlfriends Kim and Karla worked for a strip club called Seventh Heaven, and when I saw them out after work the night before, they told me, "Your little odd friend with the wild whiskers was in tonight. He stripped down, and he had bright pink bathers on underneath. He then got kicked out because he couldn't pay his bill. We were in stitches because we were bored shitless before that!" Roppongi was such a small town.

He breathed an audible sigh of relief and continued to launch into one of the craziest stories I had ever heard. According to his story, The Crow had been minding his own business on the train when two tall blonde girls approached him, asking for directions to a club in Roppongi. Being the Good Samaritan that he was, he decided to take them to the club himself, even though it was almost an hour out of his way.

While on the train, the girls whipped out enormous bottles of whiskey and encouraged him to start chugging by initiating flirty drinking games. Of course, he got utterly gooned, and as he exited the train, he thought he never had such a great train ride in his life. He ended up telling the girls that sentiment and realized they were gone. A million times worse, even through his drunken haze, he remembered offering one of the girls his jacket when she complained about being cold. That jacket was long gone and it had nearly twenty thousand dollars in it.

I wanted to stop his story and ask why the hell he had been carrying that amount of money around in his pocket, but I just let him roll with it. He needed to get it off his chest.

He then decided to go to the strip club with no money. He drank a large amount of hooch and ended up passing out in the middle of Roppongi in a pink Speedo. I could not imagine where he got it or if it was his daily choice for gitch. It was kind of funny, but I still felt sorry for him. Supposedly, the economy was not doing well and I knew that every yen he spent at the clubs came from his pocket, and from his children's mouths.

He represented the huge majority of custies who were not rich. They worked their asses off for sixteen hours a day and never spent much on themselves, besides going to exorbitant clubs.

The hostess industry could be dangerous to its clients. It was like a drug. I had already witnessed the downfall of more than one good man. I saw a client spend all his own money and start embezzling his company's money, only to be thrown into prison, a shell of his former self. It took a strong person to overcome the obsession, and The Crow did not possess a strong enough backbone.

I decided to try to do something nice for The Crow, just to make someone who has had a bad day and life feel better. That was the good thing about the hostess industry. Before I traveled to Japan, if I had seen some crazy dude passed out in the middle of the street in unflattering swimwear, I would have looked the other way. But in that place, the judged man was my friend, and I felt it was my duty to protect him. He told me he would come by the club later that week to talk and we ended the conversation.

****

I felt so drained. My energy level had run low over the last few weeks. If I were to go on, I would need a puff. I stepped out onto the balcony and sat down on my usual green plastic seat. I pulled out the silver weed grinder I had just purchased from the paraphernalia shop on the main street of Roppongi.

One of my Hawaiian girlfriends went into the same shop and was nabbed by cops when she exited with her purchases. She spent the next day in the bowels of a nasty cop shop, being interrogated and piss tested. She had done coke and weed a few days earlier, so she was happy when she came up clean and they let her go, *sans* her paraphernalia.

I waited until I was not as drunk to stake out the smoke shop. I ducked in there lightning fast when no one was around and did a mad minute shop, buying twenty packs of papers, two grinders and a lipstick case that doubled as a stash holder.

The bathroom at Jack's was always full of girls, putting on makeup or stockings or gossiping or even reading and eating. Girls would perch on ledges around the sinks and go about their business.

I had taken to piling a few girls into a stall and trying to smoke a doobie up a clogged vent hole. Of course, the room would fill up with smoke and we would get a variety of responses, some wanting in and some finding it too stinky. We would perfume it up after, but it was always pointless, as there was no ventilation in the room. The odor would linger for hours. It was risky in so many ways, but that was the way I rolled back in those days.

****

I craved danger. There was a part of me that liked Ryu's association with the mafia. It was nothing to be proud of, as the job involved cruelty and violence. And yet I imagined him as this romantic prince on a white horse, trying to save me. It was the other way around really, because he was the one that needed saving.

I felt ambivalent. On one hand, I had many amazing, talented associates. Luck was on my side when I arrived in Japan and the connections with some of the women would become lifelong friendships. One the other hand, I felt a little psychotic. Everyone had crazy urges and thoughts, but their acting on them was another story.

I was out partying every night, despite my concern for money. I began to see each customer as a profit rather than a friend or a good time. Night after night, I began relying on coke to get me in a good mood.

My positive attitude and lust for life had inspired me to my adventure in Japan, but I just wasn't feeling motivated, not when I barely saw the sun shine anymore. On top of that, I missed Weed Jesus and Svetlana something fierce. Reflecting on the way everything went down, it was unsettling. It felt unfinished.

I had crazy emotions building up inside me, and of course timing wasn't on my side. I was a total *peemiss*, a woman suffering from PMS. But it wasn't just that. So many things were weighing on my mind: Daisy, Ryu, Svetlana, my bad habits and self loathing. I was losing myself. I needed to get away.

As I sat on the patio, a small black beetle flew into view, on the railing. Every time I smoked out there, the same bug would appear and I would blow smoke at him, my constant smoking companion. I wondered if it was the same bug or if he had told his buddies about the choice *ganja* party on the fifth floor.

Whatever the case, I was happy to see him and felt a loss when he flew away. I decided right then that my own path needed to take a drastic change. I could not continue and maintain my sanity.

****

When I re-entered the kitchen, I expected everyone to be sleeping, but I encountered instead frantic mayhem that was our apartment. Diamond straddled a stool in the kitchen and yelled out, "Happy Birthday!" She held out a yummy looking breakfast, a homemade English muffin sandwich, bacon, toast, hash browns and fruit.

"The window on the balcony was open. All your smoke blew in and hot-boxed the room. When we woke up, we had the munchies in a matter of seconds," Diamond giggled, squinting her eyes. They did look a bit stoned and there was a definite haze throughout the room. Oh well, they needed to wake up anyway. Lula was finishing up the last of the cooking when I smiled over at her.

"Thanks guys!" I had completely forgotten our plan to get Tom to take us all out for a fake birthday party that night. I was just promising myself that sort of scheming would stop, and there I was, planning a fake birthday party. The idea of the gifts and money that would be mine after such a night excited me. It turned me on!

"But it's a shame to trick him. He is so nice," Lula admonished us. No matter how many scams we had, Lula refused to be a part of them. She had taken a liking to Tom straight away.

He had asked her all kinds of questions about her homeland, culture and dreams.

She liked to get drink back money as much as the rest of us, but she didn't like when we got greedy and started "playing with fire," as she put it.

"Tom is so loaded that he can fart through silk all day if he wants to. He's dying to have someone to spend his money on. Let's not let him down, now," Diamond yawned as she finished off her huge breakfast.

"It's our responsibility," Crystale deadpanned, and Amy nodded in agreement.

"Besides, Tiffany misses us and has called me numerous times. She wants in on this fake birthday, and Tom is the only custie we know who will take six champagne drinking girls on a night around town and not blink an eye," I reasoned. I missed Tiffany too. She and Justin had been taking it pretty easy, so we had not seen either of them out for a while.

"Quick! Call him, Rose," Diamond demanded.

Lula only shook her head as I dialed the number. She did not want to have any part of the scheme, but if all her girls were going to have a fake birthday party, she wasn't about to stay home and knit or whatever. Besides, she had been on the prowl and always wanted to be anywhere there might be men.

"Hi, Gorgeous," I purred into the phone. "It's your lucky day. You get to take me out for my birthday!" All the girls waited in the background in anticipation, trying to control their giggles. Diamond was already putting on shoes to run to the corner booze store. She was going to grab some bubbly for a celebration!

And so my fake birthday was arranged. Tom was only too happy to meet me for a formal dinner before the real party would begin. He loved to parade me around fancy hotel restaurants, where we were sure to be seen together.

At first I was a little embarrassed about being on a date with a man who was old enough to be my father. But as time wore on, and I went on more *dohans*, I learned to enjoy myself on those extravagant dinners.

What did I care if I received strange looks from foreigners in fancy hotels? I could change my thinking and actually enjoy the attention. At least I wasn't getting passed by without a second glance. It was their problem if they were judgers, whereas I was having a good time, and I knew damn sure my customer was having a blast too. I found my enjoyment to be of more importance than the ignorance of a few. Not that I blamed them for their assumptions. I was sure they had little knowledge of the hostess industry.

Tom showed up to dinner all smiles, with a gigantic bouquet of flowers that only added to the young hostess parade he had produced, a show that starred us. I thought I would have to chop the top off a two liter bottle of water for a makeshift vase to accommodate the blooms.

We did not own such unnecessary items as vases in our cramped apartment. There were a few worn out dishes and cooking utensils when we moved in, but we only possessed things that could be carried on our backs. Lacy underwear, beautifully crafted, delicate dresses and passports were more practical for us. We never lusted over household goods or poured over IKEA catalogues like my sister, who was eager to furnish her child's nursery.

Halfway through the most delicious duck dinner I had ever eaten at a Chinese restaurant, Tom pulled out a small box from his briefcase. In it was a gold necklace with my name, Rose Beach. Underneath the "B" was a great big rock of a diamond. I was speechless. Honestly, the diamond was of incredible size. I knew he was loaded, but I had no idea he was *such* a Mary!

"It's your birthstone, right?" he asked.

"Uh, ya." My birthstone was actually topaz, but apparently, my fake birthstone was diamond! I could definitely go with that.

"Thank you so much! This is the nicest gift I've ever received!" And it was. I had no idea how much it cost him, but I'm sure he spent a fortune. He beamed with pride and satisfaction, as one who had fulfilled his duty.

"Rose. You need better apartment. I get for you. You go to estate agent tomorrow and pick something out." With that, he asked for the check in staccato Japanese syllables, "*Okaike kudasai.*"

I had told Tom about the size and age of my battered apartment and he came through for me. As I began to thank him, he changed the subject by asking, "What doing now?"

"Wanna go sing some *karaoke*?" I asked. That question had started so many crazy nights, so I prepared myself for the party that would follow. I had hit the jackpot in terms of customers.

I perused the extensive drink menu at my favorite drink back bar and made a selection. When I ordered Crystal, the most expensive champagne on the list, he smiled and shrugged, saying, "Whatever you want."

Those words were music to my ears. I had been known to get up and leave a table if the customer started haggling over price or tried buying a cheaper bottle. Being a custie in a pricy *karaoke* club was for the rich and I did not want to waste my valuable time. On the other hand, if I was with a customer like The Crow, I would never bring him to a drink back bar, because he could not afford it. But Tom was rich.

After the first bottle of bubbly was gone and the second was well under way, I turned to Tom and said, "I have to meet my girlfriends later. But I'm having such a good time and I don't want to leave. Shall I invite them down here?" That was better than saying, in a straight way, "Five of my best girlfriends with the biggest alcohol tolerance in town are on the stampede here as we speak."

He shrugged his shoulders as if to say, "Do I have a choice?" and I was on my cell to Diamond,

"Where are you? Is Tiffany with you?" I asked.

"Ya, she's here. We're at Sheesha Bar." The loud hip-hop music coming from the other end of the receiver drowned out her voice.

"Come to *Mask*!" I yelled.

The troupe that came through the cloudy glass doors consisted of Diamond, Amy, Crystale, Lula, Tiffany and Justin, who looked drunk. I wondered what he was doing with them. Hostess evenings were typically girls only.

"Don't even ask. I could not get rid of him!" Tiffany hissed the words through her hands as she sat next to me. Justin, normally upbeat and positive, slumped next to Tiffany, depressed.

I had not seen either of them in a while. Tiffany had so many custies, since she was working on her own as a freelance hostess. She met customers on her own time and terms and brought them to the drink back clubs of her choice. She was booked solid. The custies did not have to pay club fees and they felt they weren't paying for her time when they were at "regular" places. Most custies did not know we were making money at drink back bars.

Justin looked awful. He had dark circles under his eyes and his mouth was turned down in an uncharacteristic scowl.

"What's up, Jussie?" I guffawed, trying to humor him. He was the kind of guy who did not mind us having girly nights in, painting our nails, ordering pizza and telling stories about home or traveling. In fact, he loved being with us and always weaseled his way into our parties. Because he had become one of us, we dubbed him "Jussie."

He kept scowling, at no one in particular. Finally, Tiffany turned to me with a bored sigh and said, "Justin isn't himself these days. Roppongi is getting to him." With that, Justin got up and stormed out, not looking at anyone on his way out.

"Brilliant!" Tiffany muttered. I felt for the guy. I knew things had been difficult for him. When I saw him out, he was different.

He seemed jaded, but who could blame him? He was a Tout, and that meant standing out on the streets rain or shine, approaching random people trying to get them to come into a club. It really took a certain coolness and cynicism to do that job well. Potential customers could sense desperation a mile away and Justin had to walk a fine between being respectful and being pushy.

It was difficult for a guy in Roppongi. Girls had the advantage. We ran the show. The customers would go where the girls wanted and do what they wanted. If a guy could not speak Japanese or he did not have a post-secondary education, he could teach English, do illegal business, be employed as a waiter, Tout or bartender. There were not many options. It must have been difficult for a guy to watch his girlfriend go out with many different men and come home with money and expensive gifts he could not afford to give.

The lure and appeal of becoming a Roppongi gangster was real, and because of it, I was worried for Justin. He was acting like Weed Jesus, so I decided to talk to Tiffany. I thought it was time for them to do something different. They had devised many elaborate schemes and plans together. I wanted them to act on those.

Tom was clueless about what happened between Tiff and Justin, as his attention was devoted to "yours truly." To say that he liked me would be a huge understatement. He could not wait to fill my champagne glass and gaze longingly at me as I sang *karaoke*.

And Lula was right. He was nice. I understood why girls could have sugar daddies. I imagined myself living the high life, but then reality bit me in the ass as I imagined myself shagging Tom. The fantasy evaporated as I envisioned his wrinkled face above mine, his soft, repulsive body humping away for all it was worth. That vision was all I needed to sober me.

I had a choice to make. Until then, I had never led a customer on or given one the girl friend, or GFE experience. I could either collect my winnings and bow out gracefully or go "all in." I was tired of the song and dance that I was expected to perform as a hostess. Right then, I decided to fold from the hostess game. I was done. So I ordered two more bottles and went home. There I would plan my escape from Tokyo and from the hostess industry.

Loud, hip-hop music woke me from my dream the next morning. The nastiness of that particular hangover interfered with my sleep, as I awoke with a familiar feeling of falling fast and far. Realizing I was halfway between dream and sleep, I mustered my strength and woke up. I had the dream again, the one where Ryu pushed me off the cliff. While I wondered what it meant, my head began to pound like a bad bass line as a feeling of *déjà vu* overwhelmed me.

The smell of bacon reached my nostrils and my abused stomach turned over with a sickly gurgle. I opened one eye a crack, and saw the girls spread out, with Lula cooking breakfast. The girls were already awake and sat about in various states of nakedness.

"Can you believe she actually snogged Tom last night?" Diamond giggled. Everyone had a good chuckle, me included. *God, someone must have been really drunk to have kissed Tom!* I wondered who it was.

"I thought that I was going to piss myself when she jumped on him and started singing all those raunchy hip-hop songs," Tiffany whispered hoarsely from behind me. I had not noticed she was even there. Come to think of it, I did not even remember coming home on that night.

"I can't believe that Tom is going to buy you a house, Lula!" Amy exclaimed in an amazed voice.

I had to get up. My curiosity was just too great. As I sat up, stretching, everyone fixed their attention on me.

"There's the woman of the hour!" Tiffany exclaimed, in great spirits.

"I am so hung it's not even funny," I moaned. "I can't remember anything past like the fifth bottle of Crystal."

"That's too bad, but since I have pictures and videos, we can refresh your memory," Tiffany joked.

"You don't!" gasped Crystale. After looking at the pictures and videos, a sane person could only come to one conclusion. *I was a girl gone bad!*

The camera was too honest for my liking. There was picture after picture of me, singing *karaoke* with crazed expressions, and my makeup awry. I saw a video of me jumping from stall to stall, grabbing Tom's tie and putting on a dominatrix type show, which did not paint a virtuous picture of me.

And last, but definitely not least, I had kissed Tom. I had to admit I was ashamed of myself. Of course I loved having a good time, but seeing those pictures the next day kind of hit home.

Being honest with myself, I had acted like those *skebbae* hostesses I did not respect. Not only that, but I was in love with another man. Jealousy was a bitter pill to swallow. I tortured myself, and as I imagined Ryu's desirable lips interlocked with someone else's lips, I was eaten up with jealousy. *What had I done?*

Looking at Lula, I noticed she was the only one not laughing. I watched a big fat tear roll down her cheek. Crystale noticed right away, putting her arm around Lula and comforting her.

"What's wrong?" she asked.

"Oh, I'm not sad. I'm happy," she sighed. "I cry tears of joy now. My family will have home. I don't believe it!"

Crystale saw my blank face and realized the night had been a total blackout for me.

"Tom told us last night that he was going to put you in a nicer apartment," she said. "Then you started going off about how Lula needed a house and that she only needed about forty thousand dollars for a down payment. You were really persuasive and he agreed, Rose. You should have been a lawyer!"

As I looked into Lula's ecstatic face, I realized I had one more duty to perform as a hostess. I was not done. I needed to get Lula a house.

LULA'S HOUSE

The day after Justin stormed out of the bar, he and Tiffany had one of their long talks. They had cried it out and discovered they had more issues to work through than they thought, especially considering their jobs. Justin had already been checking out commercial real estate properties on the Caribbean coast with a Costa Rican surfer buddy.

Pooling money together, Justin and Tiffany had more than enough to buy tickets to Costa Rica and open a bar right on the beach. So they picked up the phone, called their travel agent and made a life changing decision. They described it as "freeing." They were leaving for good. It was a bittersweet farewell. We all supported their decision, realizing they needed to move on with their lives, beyond Japan.

We had enjoyed so many escapades and fabulous times together. I was going to miss them. They were always encouraging my music, offering positive feedback when I shared the start of a song or a poem. Friends like them were hard to come by and we were determined to maintain our friendship across an ocean.

So we did what we did best. We had a stinking crazy party and got the two of them smashed, Roppongi style, for the last time. I was depressed when they left. I missed their support. Whenever we sang *karaoke*, they would pick song after song for me to sing and they would always applaud the loudest. Tiffany was forever urging me to perform at an open mike night, but I wanted to write more new material first.

Crystale and Amy moved into their apartment after Tiffany left. It was fun living together, but closet space was limited, and they were tired of living out of suitcases. Only Diamond, Lula and I remained in the apartment, but Diamond was getting antsy. She was easily bored.

It might have been different if she had a man there. Many of the long term girls were either married or had a steady boyfriend. Diamond was enjoying her status as a single woman, though it had been too long since she had been laid. She seemed irritated all the time.

The cool thing about the old Diamond was her enjoyment of life and freedom from needing a man. She was too interested in dancing and partying with us to even notice if there were any cute guys around. In my experience, desperation never worked. A decent man could smell desperation a mile away.

Diamond announced she was leaving Tokyo a week after Tiffany and Justin left, and I was not surprised. Sapphire's baby was due in a little over a month, and she wanted to be there for her best friend. She decided to visit Sapphire for a month and help out with the baby before flying back to Australia. She already had a line on a topless waitressing gig in Melbourne.

Things were starting to change in Roppongi. Ten years before, foreign hostesses seemed far more rare, but now there were so many clubs and so many beautiful girls that we were working in a flooded market. I was lucky to have the good custies I did. I was still a new hostess, compared to girls who had been there for years and knew all the customers. Diamond was not leaving just because she was bored. She did not want to have to solicit men to take her out, when doing that was necessary to make money. Beyond that, the kind of custie who would give a hostess the big bucks would require a hardcore GFE.

I understood what was happening. People were realizing, if even on a sub-conscious level, a weird energy in Roppongi. Everyone was flying the coop, jumping ship with the rats, and fast. I was not the martyr type, so I followed suit. I had not been born in the year of the sheep for nothing.

****

I missed Canada. I wanted to be there for the birth of my niece. Daisy lived in Vancouver. As soon as she graduated from high school, she got away from the prairies as quickly as possible. Our small hometown had become stifling in our few years there. It was teeming with racism and patriotic illness. It was not a good place to develop as an artist or person. Our town boasted twice as many churches as restaurants. And while it was interesting to be part of a small community and know everyone, we longed to see the world.

Daisy yearned to be near the ocean and to feel the cool breeze on her face. She liked the mild, summertime weather. Saskatchewan, where we grew up, was called the land of the living sky and was in the Midwest of Canada.

Throughout the year, we experienced the most dangerous, unpredictable storms, while we watched in fear, behind the safety of our small glass windows. We had the opportunity to behold the most glorious Northern lights and gaze at rows of brightly colored, patchwork fields. There was no doubting the natural beauty, but we were so bent on travel that these awe inspiring sights were wasted on our eyes.

For the first time in our lives, we were apart as twins. I was devastated when she left, but I was in love with my high school sweetheart, and I loved hard. I would have done anything to be with him, even if it meant moving to a nearby hockey city where he could pursue his goals. I was not qualified to do anything but wait tables, so I got a job at a sports bar, thinking our love would be enough to keep us happy.

After a year went by, I wondered if I would be anything more than someone's girlfriend. My inner voice shouted that I needed a change. I always wanted to be a musician and wanted to be somewhere I could pursue music. Each day became more of a struggle as the voice became louder, urging me to take action and to get out.

When I finally got the courage to tell my boyfriend I was moving to Vancouver, we cried all night. Sometimes love was not enough to keep people together, and I believed our paths had crossed for a reason. We had learned from each other.

But I needed more. I had something to prove to the world and to those who doubted my abilities. I needed to show those people that I was a serious musician and they had missed out for not giving me a chance. It took years to learn their acceptance did not matter.

I did not want merely to exist. That was not enough. I needed to be remembered, and I wanted to create a legacy of my own, something physical like a CD of my works. As I sat on a bus bound for Vancouver, I watched my first love walk away, his muscular frame fading into the distance. I knew I would never see him again.

Over time, I began with my music, going to open mike nights and approaching selected artists for collaboration ideas. I started writing songs and capturing emotions that I did not know I even had. Writing became therapeutic, rather than a means to an end.

****

As I sat in Tokyo, reflecting on my time in Canada, I missed writing music. I did not feel like myself. My life had become a series of parties I barely remembered in a single purpose to fill my bank account. I decided not to tell anyone about my plans to return to Vancouver and rather focus on the task at hand – Lula's house.

Yes, Tom told me that he was going to buy Lula a house, but I wanted to approach the subject in a roundabout way so I would not scare him off. For the next few weeks, I launched a campaign to raise forty thousand dollars. That was all Lula needed to pay the deposit on a home for her and her family. I hung a blackboard on the wall, on which I wrote in large, bold letters, "GET $40,000 OFF TOM!"

When I woke each morning, I would text him, "Good Morning. Hope you had a good sleep." I would ask him detailed questions about his day and listen to him to remember which meetings he had on what days.

We went on many *dohans*, and not once did I ask him to take me to an expensive *karaoke* bar. In fact, I did not take him out for drink backs during the first month. If my calculations were correct, he usually spent at least five thousand dollars every time we went on a date. That meant if I asked him for forty thousand dollars after a month, it wasn't such a crazy request.

He took me to dinners at restaurants in trendy hotels, where everyone could see us as I bided my time. I was giving him the *Girl Friend Experience*. That was the only way things would work out. And work it did. After our fourth date, I straight up asked him to give me the forty grand. He told me he would have it for me by the next day.

I could not sleep all that night. The thought of Lula getting her house money was exhilarating. Everything seemed better in the world. And even though I hustled my way into getting the money, it did not diminish the high.

Something occurred to me just then. I realized I had become even more addicted to attaining money. I told myself I would ditch Tom after the scheme. I did not want to play with his emotions, and I was tired of giving him the *Girl Friend Experience.*

My phone beeped, letting me know I had a text message. I knew it was from Tom. The text read, "I love you." *Shit!* The next few months were a whirlwind. I had a gorgeous brand new apartment right in the center of Azabu Juban. It was a great neighborhood, with delectable bakeries, busy coffee shops and a steady stream of foreigners and Japanese people.

Lula went back to Estonia a different woman. She was poised and self-assured. Confident, she had started to experiment with makeup and clothing, trying to get a fashion sense of herself. She confided she wanted to become a nurse and use her savings to go back to school.

We were on our way back to Narita. Her visa would not expire for a month, but she had scored in Roppongi. I envied her and realized that I could just hop the next flight back to Vancouver if I wanted. But I could not have left Japan, leaving so much unfinished and unfulfilled.

And what about Ryu? He had not so much as emailed me in the past month, and my pride would not allow me to contact him. I wondered if he was still abroad. More importantly was the question: *did he give a shit about me?*

As Tom became more obsessed with me, my days and nights became filled with the drudgery of a fake relationship. I ignored my other custies and stopped going in to work because a night out with Tom would earn me more money than a week at Jack's.

Asking Tom for money and gifts became easy. I had already saved thirty thousand dollars in a Canadian bank account. After Tom's gifts, I had another fifty thousand dollars sitting in my freezer, waiting for me to bank. With each day that went by, I woke up later and later. The banks closed at three p.m. in Japan, so I would always miss them.

I liked having such a fat stash of cash. It was flamboyant. Every so often I would take all the cold *ichimans* out, fan myself with them and take pictures. I was obsessed with money. *Why should I have stopped there, when I could get five hundred thousand dollars and have enough to buy a house?*

One day when we were at dinner, Tom suggested we should go away together. "I go to Thailand next month? You come?" he asked, while gazing at me.

I almost choked on my *unagi* sushi. I had learned to eat many different foods in Japan. Before I went, I would have never dreamed of eating eel or fermented soybeans. I forced myself to be adventurous and to try the exotic, delicious cuisine of Japan. I loved it. However, there were some Japanese delicacies that did not work for me, like grilled cow's tongue and blowfish testicles.

Until then, Tom let me get away with extravagances. We went shopping at high-end boutiques, like Louis Vuitton and Chanel every other weekend. My wardrobe was phenomenal. I had a bag and luggage collection to die for and my enormous shoe closet only had enough space to hold my shoes for each season. I had to put the rest of them away in storage. My apartment was stunning and huge by Japanese standards, with gorgeous views of the city.

In short, I was living the high life and I had not even kissed him again. Yet try as I might, I could not imagine us on a trip together. And if I allowed myself to think about it, I was not proud of the life I was living. During the previous month, I tried to envision a life with that rich older man. And in those days, my vision was clouded.

I *deserved* a man I loved! And I just did not love in Tom that way. To give up my money addiction cold turkey would be a challenge. I needed to trust myself to believe I could provide for my own future. My obsession with possessions only satisfied my greed temporarily before they lost their appeal.

So I had another choice to make. Tom's eager face assured me I could be a kept woman and never want for anything again. *Wasn't that the reason I came to Japan?* I wondered. *Wasn't it to gain financial independence?* It was a rare moment of clarity.

I was grateful for all the things I had: an amazing family back home, so many great friends in Japan, my health, my youth, my talent, and a future worth living. I was sick of trying to please people. I did not know I was so emotional about it, but I was ready to explode, like a volcano. I was getting angry. Not just for me, but for all the girls throughout the world who were stuck in loveless relationships.

But it was not fair to make Tom the victim of my growing rage. He was actually a great guy, though he liked girls half his age. And who could blame him? There were pictures of half naked, young girls with blank stares and lingering pouts displayed all over Japan.

And he, like most men who frequented clubs, was in an unhappy marriage. It was the result of a society that pressured people to marry too early. Marriage was mandatory if a man wanted respect, especially in Japan's business world. The main purpose of a man's life was to get a good job and to get married. That was it. But there was no importance placed on fulfilling dreams, self-exploration, or traveling and experiencing new cultures.

The older generation was robbed of the chance to be themselves, something I took for granted, That was the only reason I could fathom why an intelligent, kind and successful man like Tom would chase and spend money on a young woman he most likely knew did not love him. He was chasing his lost youth.

Summoning the courage to look him in the eyes, I replied, "No, Tom. I think it's better if you go by yourself." He was crestfallen. I really hated to hurt his feelings and I struggled, trying to find the right words to say. Just then, the waiter came over, and we were both grateful for the well timed interruption.

As we exited, I waited until he placed me in a taxi and gave me the last *ichiman* he would ever give me for taxi fare. It was a generous final gesture, typical of a classy man. In the rear-view mirror, I watched him standing there alone, and I felt a tinge of shame for causing him pain.

But I finally felt free. For the first time in months, a familiar trickle of excitement made its way down my spine. I recognized it as the need to travel.

"Do you know an *onsen* outside Tokyo?" I asked the cab driver. There was no answer from the front seat, except a blank glance in my direction from the rear view mirror. He could not speak a word of English.

"*Onsen, Tokyo toi, Kudasai.*" I fumbled with the few Japanese words I knew. I had just said, "Hot Springs. Tokyo far away, please."

"*Doko desuka?*" he asked. "Where?"

Good question. I honestly had no idea. I had to think. After a few tense seconds, I remembered the name of the place Crystale had been to the previous weekend.

"*Yamanishi?*" I asked, hesitating. I hoped that was right. I only remembered the name because the first part sounds like a Rasta saying, "*Ya mon!*"

"*Yama*nashi?" he roared, incredulous. "*Honto?*"

"*Honto*," I answered nodding, telling him that "yes," it was true, I wanted to go to Yamanashi. He gave me one last pleading glance in the rear-view, as if to say, "What did I do to deserve this?" And we were off.

YAMANASHI

The drive to Yamanashi took almost two hours. As the city lights disappeared behind me, I felt my worries drift away, at one with the fading light. The temperature was pleasant, so I asked the driver to turn off the air conditioner. I wanted to enjoy the crisp air.

I could tell the driver thought I was insane. I had made him stop at my apartment so I could grab a few things, namely my weed stash, my passport and cash. As an afterthought, I grabbed the female cat figurine that had been a symbol of Weed Jesus and Svetlana's love. I placed it in the special pocket of my suitcase. I missed my friends like crazy. I could not linger on thoughts about them, as my cab was waiting. I needed that trip.

I opened the freezer door and surveyed the pile of cash in one corner. I chided myself for not depositing that fat stack in my bank account. I figured I could do it when I got back. I grabbed twenty thousand dollars and left.

It may have been way too much for the trip, but I did not know if they would have bank machines in the boonies of Japan. I had no idea how much money I would spend when I was away. Leaving thirty thousand dollars, I closed the freezer and ran back outside to my taxi.

Settling down for the hour and a half taxi ride, the cab driver began to smile at me, as if trying to figure out my story. He seemed a little worried. On one hand, he was happy because he was going to make at least five hundred dollars on the taxi ride, while on the other he was probably worried that he was helping me escape in some sort of heist or other criminal activity.

The mountains welcomed me like old friends. As I glanced at them through the fading dusk, the spindly trees along their slopes made them look like big, furry creatures. The farther we drove, the calmer I became. I was running away in essence. *But running from what and to where?* It mattered less with every kilometer I traveled away from Tokyo.

Crystale had described the *onsen,* a traditional hot springs, as an incredible experience. The baths were ornate, though they were made from natural materials, like stone and bamboo. The water was meant to heal the mind and body. Many were outdoors.

I told the taxi driver I wanted to go to an *onsen* hotel. He dropped me off in front of a gorgeous little place, complete with a tiny, *ukata*-clad older woman who bowed when we drove up. She tried to carry my bags, but I felt it would be a challenge, so I insisted on grabbing them myself.

The room was exactly what I hoped for, a traditional style Japanese room. The bamboo *tatami* mats were freshly swept, and in the center of the room, there sat a low black table, with two matching high backed seats on the ground, facing each other.

The gray haired woman from the front entered and gestured to me, indicating that I should put on the maroon colored robe and pink cotton belt, folded in the closet. I wondered where I would sleep, but I saw a thin futon and a warm looking blanket when she opened the closet. I guessed I would make my bed later.

When she left, I puffed a dube and went down to the *onsen*. Some *onsens* had a private bath right in the room, but they were one thousand dollars a night and up, while mine was closer to two hundred. I jumped the stairs, two at a time, and made my way down to the *onsen*.

Standing before two entrances to two separate *onsens*, I felt like the girl in the movie *Labyrinth*. But unlike the movie, there was not a soul to be seen or anyone to ask which door to choose. A blue curtain, with a slit opening the middle, adorned the first entry way, while an identical curtain in red adorned the second. I knew the *kanji* for man and woman, but for the life of me, I could not remember it. I tried the red, hoping I would not get an eyeful of some dude's scrotum.

As I opened the door, I was relieved to find the bath was empty. I still did not know if I was in the correctly-gendered *onsen*, but that did not stop me from getting stark naked. I was not disappointed when I entered the sanctuary of the empty bath house. A small waterfall tumbled down black stone walls into an enormous raw cedar tub. I noticed a sliding glass door and realized there was an outside area.

Stepping outside, my bare feet, which had not felt earth and grass for months, tingled with excitement. Before getting in the bath, I remembered Crystale's advice about washing the body before getting in the tub. There were individual bath stations, and each was equipped with a low stool, various soaps and a dousing bucket. After I was squeaky clean, I sat down on the crude wooden ledge and slid into the waiting water, letting out an audible sigh.

Whatever my future held, I was happy and grateful for that simple moment. *Thank you, Creator!* I was not a slave to my phone. I was enjoying myself on my terms, and I was happy in my own company. I did not need anyone.

Just then, the wind started to pick up and ruffle my hair, warning of an eminent storm. When cold raindrops began to fall on my head, the heat of the medicinal pool kept me comfortable. I only left that beautiful scene when I started getting sleepy. So I dried off, wrapped myself in the cotton robe and cinched my waist with the rose-colored belt. I headed to my room, only to find the futon ready and waiting.

At seven o'clock the next morning, I was awakened by a light tapping at the door. It was the proprietor, the older woman, and she wanted to come in and take my futon away and bring me breakfast. I could not remember the last time I had been up so early.

But I was not put out by the early hour and I ate the breakfast, making sure that I ate all my pickles and each grain of rice. She nodded in approval as she watched me eat. I suspected it was about as much emotion as I would see out of the stoic lady.

Still I was curious and I wanted to try my limited Japanese in speaking with her. "*Anato no namae wa nan desuka*?" I asked, showing my lack of imagination by asking her name.

"*Makiko*," she answered, seeming taken aback because I spoke Japanese.

After that, we had a limited conversation, during which I recognized I should learn more Japanese if I wanted to travel outside Tokyo. I had studied almost every afternoon by myself, but I needed to be in a class environment to become more fluent.

She told me where to go sightseeing and called a taxi to take me where I wanted to go. Later that afternoon, I visited a sacred place that had crystals of various shapes and sizes. Some were even bigger than I was. And on the way down from there, I saw forests and waterfalls cascading down mountains. The rest of the day was filled with natural beauty I never expected to see in Japan. It made me love the country all the more.

The driver was a friendly, blue-eyed Japanese guy named Masa, with a crazy surfer tan. He spoke some English. He took me to an amazing *soba* restaurant, where I insisted on buying both of us the best *soba* I had ever tasted.

Outside the window, I noticed a table next to a Japanese maple tree. Next to the tree sat a girl with an empty bowl, nursing a delicate cup of green tea. Her windblown hair reminded me of Svetlana. I rushed outside, vainly expecting her to be there.

The girl turned, distracted from her thoughts, and smiled at me. Her almond-shaped eyes were quick and intelligent as she gestured for me to join her.

"*Haaiii.* I'm Yuko." She had a hoarse, playful voice.

"*Haaiii.* I'm Rose," I echoed. I noticed a small guitar case resting by her leg, next to the table. "You play?" I asked.

"Yes, I play stage tonight. You come?" she asked and flashed me a thumbs up sign. I guessed her English level was on par with my Japanese. Our corresponding vocabularies were pitiful, but we understood each other and had no trouble communicating.

"Okay, *jusho kudasai.*" I asked her for the address in Japanese so she would know I was trying to speak her language. As I thought about it, I never had any real Japanese girlfriends before. I spent my time in the hostess industry, having a life that revolved around men. *Right there was an opportunity!*

Masa would take me to Yuko's gig later that night, after I had a chance to enjoy a feast and *onsen.* I expected a coffee shop type venue when I dressed for the evening, since it was such a sleepy town. Being fresh from Tokyo, I had few casual clothes.

I felt a lot more comfortable in flattering, bling evening wear than in comfortable, practical clothing. So I went all out on my outfit, wearing tight fitting, dark blue denim jeans, a flashy belt and a hot pink, off the shoulder T-shirt. I wore my hair down and curly. A pair of fake eyelashes and black sparkly nail polish completed the look.

I strutted over to where Masa indicated. It seemed like the right place, but all I could see was a hip-hop club with a bunch of serious, gangster type Japanese guys in front of it. I glanced back at Masa with uncertainty and was about to return to the car when I heard my name being called.

From behind me, a young Japanese girl approached the car. Every guy in front of the club stopped and stared at her, and with good reason. She was wearing one of the most sexy, cool, scandalous outfits I had ever seen! Yuko was wearing Kos Play, or costume play.

She strutted past the guys like she did not see them and snarled at one, saying something in guttural Japanese. She seemed to be comparing him to a pig. In reaction, they looked away, trying to appear busy.

I was in awe as she continued across the street in five-inch black stilettos. Even Masa was distracted. She wore a purple plaid bikini that wrapped around her body, fishnet stockings, and a garter belt. She had individual diamantes glued on her arms and face, and her hair was pulled up on the side, exposing her half shaven head. Best of all, she had a colorful crane tattooed down the side of her tiny abdomen and inner thigh.

She seemed a different girl earlier. Judging by her fabulous getup, I knew she was an artist.

"You look amazing!" I gushed as I saw her. She looked at me and smiled, not understanding a word I said, but neither of us cared at that point. She grabbed my arm, like I was her possession, and we went into the club, ready for action.

Halfway into the night, we smoked a fatty that I prepared for the occasion, but I had vowed never to do coke again. The dirty high and the horrible come-down were enough to make me quit it. I had a great time without it and I did not need another destructive vice in my life.

When Yuko went on stage later that night, magic happened. Because she had a guitar, I expected her to play folk music or soft rock, but she got on stage and started singing original songs that were heartfelt reggae fusion music. She had a full band backing her up, and halfway through one of the songs, two petite Japanese girls got on stage and started gyrating to the beat, *hood rat* style. One even got on her head and started shaking her ass around violently. Her legs looked like helicopter propellers on springs, kicking about.

You could tell that Yuko's show was a crowd favorite, and she had everyone mesmerized. She spoke in Japanese, but I found myself laughing along with everyone else over her crazy antics on stage. She would break out in choreographed dances they all knew and made crude gestures to the audience. She even pulled one happy looking guy on stage and placed her heel on is temple, while yelling and whipping him with a chain.

 At the end of the set, she played a sweet Japanese ballad on her guitar, alone under the spotlight. Her raspy voice made even the most rowdy guys in the house silent. Then it was pandemonium. People applauded as she bowed and jumped off the stage. She was mauled by her adoring fans. We danced our asses off for the rest of the night, on and off the bar.

 Standing on the bar, I saw a small VIP area across the smoky room and felt like chilling there. I pointed out the area to Yuko and gestured I was going there. Yuko waved at me, so I headed off in search of a place to rest.

 I plunked myself down on the soft velour sofa and surveyed the scene. I was not too drunk, as I had been trying to get my high on the music, dancing and partying. My mood changed as I looked to my left and saw two men yelling at each other over the blaring music.

 I could not tell what they were saying, but the exchange was heated. The one facing me would have been handsome, if it were not for his distorted countenance. I could see the veins in his neck bulging under his starched white shirt as he tried to intimidate the other man.

 He became aware of my scrutiny and turned, staring at me. The expression on his face sent a chill down my spine, but it changed so quickly I thought I must have imagined it. When he smiled, he seemed to recognize me. I thought he looked familiar as well, but I could not figure out how I knew him. I averted his glance, pretending not to notice, while I racked my brain trying to remember.

 Then it came to me. The burly guy was Diamond's ex-boyfriend, Damian. I had only met him once, but from what Diamond told me, once was enough. Not only was he a bad lay, he was rough during sex. He did not want her to talk at all, but *he* loved to talk nasty to her and call her dirty names. She loved his body and the fact that he was a K-1 fighter, but his sadistic behavior turned her off.

 Damian was also involved in many illegal businesses. Because he was half Japanese and half Italian, as well as a K-1 fighter, he was well respected. The Japanese mafia trusted him, and his reputation as being untouchable was well known in Roppongi clubs.

Diamond was afraid to break it off because he was so powerful, but she finally confided in Sato-san, and he took care of it. Damian was not allowed anywhere near Diamond after Sato was through with him. From what I heard, he held a grudge against Sato-san and Diamond after that. I saw him out with a bevy of gorgeous girls on his arms a few times since then, but his eyes always seemed to fixate on me. *I got the feeling he lusted after me.*

Weed Jesus knew how cruel Damian was, too. On one occasion after we became friends, he shared a disturbing story. During a coke deal at Jesus' apartment, Damian was left alone in the room for a few minutes. After he returned, he discovered one of his pet birds was missing. He questioned Damian, who was oblivious and indifferent as to the bird's whereabouts. Sometime later, Jesus found his favorite bird outside his window, crushed to death. Damian could lie without conscious.

With all those thoughts circling in my mind, he approached me from across the room. As he was about to sit down, he motioned to his friends. Before I knew it, two thugs swooped forward and grabbed the man who was arguing with him.

That was the distraction I needed to make my swift escape. I did not want to be in the same room with the man, let alone pretend to be polite if he talked to me. I was almost out the door, and seeking the safety of my *onsen*, when I heard a familiar voice. It stopped me dead in my tracks.

"She's mine."

It was the man being dragged from the club. The men who flanked him stopped for a second and allowed him to step into the light. I turned in slow motion, as if in a dream, to see Ryu.

For long, agonizing months, I tried in vain to forget about him. As I looked into his chocolate eyes, I realized I was still in love with him. I was livid about his lack of communication, but his timing was impeccable. If there was ever a situation where I needed him to save me, the time had come.

As I surveyed the scene however, I realized that *he* was the one who needed to be saved and I found the situation humorous. It was typical for my life. If I wanted anything done right, I would have to do it myself.

A few minutes earlier, I did not feel I had the courage to stand up to Damian. But out of necessity, I formed a plan within seconds. Damian was a predator, and I was his prey. I could see the hunger in his eyes. When he realized Ryu was interested in me, it made him want me all the more. Damian did not detect the emotions, raging inside me, so I played along and gave him a doe-eyed look. I took his hand in mine and ran my fingers along his arm.

"I am nobody's! I'm certainly not yours!" I scoffed at Ryu, unleashing all of my anger toward him. I was afraid my performance was a little too convincing. Before I could kick it down a notch, Damian pulled me back, squeezing hard. As he leaned in for a kiss, I turned my face to one side, pretending to stumble.

"Oops!" I whimpered and grabbed onto a table, trying to appear feeble. Ryu acted betrayed. For a moment, a pathetic part of me enjoyed seeing him look dejected. Thank God survival mode took over. I had to take a chance if we were going to make it out of there... alive.

Since that poor Aussie girl was raped in Roppongi, I carried my smuggled pepper spray around everywhere I went. It made me feel less apprehensive about walking home alone or being in potentially dangerous environments. I felt a surge of raw adrenaline as I ripped the can out of my pocket and sprayed Damian directly in the eyes, at close range.

His screams caught his goons off guard, long enough for me to start directing the stream toward them. While they were blinded by the spray, I looked around for Ryu and the exit. I did not expect to hear the sound of metal, as a shiny gun hit the ground next to my feet.

I had not held a gun since my youth on the farm, and I had not missed it in the least. Guns had never been cool for me. I did not relish the thought of the damage they could inflict. But at that moment, I was grateful I knew how to use one. I leveled the gun in one hand and took steady aim at the men who were preoccupied with pain.

I grabbed Ryu with my other hand, and somehow managed to help him off the floor. He could barely see. During the mayhem, some of the pepper spray residue must have gotten into his eyes.

"We will find you, Bitch! I'll get both of you!" we heard Damian scream as he scrambled to get up and follow us. I had come to Yamanashi to get away from all the drama, but that situation was a million times worse than any before.

Yuko was near the door, watching my frantic escape as I clung to Ryu, struggling to get away. She seemed confused and frozen with terror. I hoped I would see her again so that I could explain everything.

We hurried into the night toward a nearby parking lot. He tossed me his keys. When I clicked the button, a white Mercedes lit up and made a soft beeping sound.

It was the first time that I had ever driven in Japan, and it would be down the pitch black streets of Yamanashi. I was not used to driving on the left side of the road and had no idea where I was going. Ryu could not give me directions, as his vision was still blurred. For someone who prided herself on being a defensive driver, I drove like a speed demon through the winding streets.

It felt amazing to see the man I loved again, never mind that we were in the middle of a car chase. The thought of living without Ryu seemed unbearable, although it was possible those feelings would not be reciprocated.

Just as I was sorting out my feelings, I caught the flash of a single headlight closing in on us. We were being followed. I sped up the car and started careening around corners at dangerous speeds. I feared for our lives, thinking one false move could bring certain death. The sides of the road were sheer cliffs that went straight down.

But if I thought I was driving fast, then whoever was following us was a maniac! A sleek black motorcycle pulled alongside our car as I looked toward Ryu in utter terror, wondering what would happen to us. I would have to ram this guy off the road if I wanted us to survive.

But then I noticed long, flowing black hair, garter belt and stockings. It was Yuko! I stopped and pulled over to the side of the road. Yuko was off her bike in an instant, with a rage in her eyes I had never seen before in another person. She leapt at Ryu and pounded his chest with her closed fists.

"Wait!" I screamed. It all happened so fast that I hardly had time to jump in and save Ryu from the wrath of Yuko, who had begun to claw his face. "She doesn't know you! Explain to her what's going on!" I begged Ryu.

Ryu spat out a string of quick Japanese words and a name: "Damian." Yuko seemed to understand right away. Ryu explained to me that she thought I was being kidnapped and her first instinct was to follow us.

****

The Yamanashi Mountains turned out to be our sanctuary, comprised of winding pathways, strategic lookout points and hidden lairs. Yuko followed us to one of those hideouts. From what I could discern in the darkness, it was a small house, concealed behind a long driveway, surrounded by dense foliage. It seemed like an ordinary cabin, until we entered.

I was surprised by how cool it was inside! There were turntables lining the main wall of the house. Hundreds of vinyl records in plastic boxes stood stacked on top of each other. There was a small shelf stocked with weed paraphernalia, Japanese cook books, and expensive, hand cut glassware.

It was a good thing I had brought money. The crime rate in Japan was low, so I did not think twice about bringing that huge wad of cash with me. I also brought my passport. At least I had a way *out* of Japan. My visa was to end in a few weeks and I did not plan on overstaying it.

I was thankful I was wearing the pewter cat that hung almost to my waist, suspended from a golden sinew. I thought of it as a good luck charm. The three of us entered the room and plopped down on the trashed sofa. Ryu was recovering from the pepper spray, but I figured it would take a while.

OUR LIVES FOREVER CHANGED

As we sat there, Yuko and Ryu spoke Japanese, without any effort to include me. The lumpy sofa felt luxurious to me and I drifted off, as my friends' familiar and comforting voices lulled me to sleep.

The sun was a brilliant orb on the horizon, like in a fairy tale. A tiny girl played alone on the shoreline, her black chiffon dress getting salted and wet as she ran along the beach. Only she seemed so small to be all alone. She must have realized her solitude as she whispered a pathetic whimper, looking around for her trusted loved ones.

Her cry was answered by a strong, older man who came along and scooped her up, singing to her an ancient song. Alarmed by what he saw, the man ran the girl back to a garden, where her mother and father waited anxiously, behind the protection of an enormous glass wall.

The silver in his hair glistened in the sun and the world seemed to stop. He seemed content as he started to walk toward the safety of the wall.

In that moment, I realized the older man was Sato-san. *Just then, a massive wave in the shape of a hand came from behind him, and I watched in horror as he was carried out to sea.*

****

I woke up in a cold sweat, disoriented. The dream chilled me to the bone, and I was convinced it was ominous. My twin and I shared strange dreams from the time we were little girls, and they always meant something.

I was lying on a comfortable futon, wearing only my undies. Someone had undressed me. I looked around for Ryu and saw him sleeping at my left, on his own futon. He must have sensed I was awake, because I watched his eyelids lift one at a time. After a few minutes, he sat straight up, fixing me with his stare.

"Goo morning." He had not learned how to enunciate his words. It was sexy and endearing.

"Where's Sato-san?" I asked. He was taken aback that I would ask about Sato-san before anything else.

"Look, I had a weird dream and..." I began.

"What *kind* of dream?" he interrupted.

I was hoping he would not press me for details. He adored Sato-san and I did not want to add to his pain. The dream was final in my mind, but I felt compelled to tell him everything.

As I told him about my dream, the blood drained from his face and he turned pale. He looked away, and withdrew to his own thoughts, but I refused to let him close me out again.

"Tell me what happened!" I demanded. The story Ryu wove involved him and Sato-san running from the Japanese mafia, in four different countries, seeking shelter in the homes of Sato's girlfriends.

Sato owed millions of dollars to dangerous thugs. They were bloodthirsty and did not take well to being cheated. It was a matter of pride and respect for them rather than money. They waited for Sato-san to come back to Japan. It was only a matter of time. His lavish spending habits were hard to break. His fate was sealed. When he ran out of cash, his only option was to return.

When he and Ryu arrived, they went into hiding at one of the secret cabins. They were back for a week when one night Ryu, feeling pent-up, went for a walk. He returned to find the cabin under siege, with the numbers and firepower against him. He could do no more than watch as the men inside confronted Sato-san and led him out to the car.

Three men in dark clothing and sunglasses took orders from a tall, stocky man. Ryu wanted to intervene, but there was nothing he could do for Sato-san, at least not at that moment. It was the last time Ryu saw the old man.

Ryu recognized the man who was giving orders. It was Damian. Ryu and Damian were well acquainted. In fact, they were best friends as teenagers. The friendship end ended when Ryu went to work for Sato-san, who was the bitter rival of Damian's boss.

Because he was Sato-san's right-hand man, Ryu knew the mafia would also be looking for him. A sensible man would have taken the little money he had and gotten the hell out of Japan, but Ryu possessed a keen sense of loyalty and honor.

He knew the only way to save Sato-san was to appeal the former friendship and Damian's own sense of honor, if it even existed. Of course, Damian just laughed and told Ryu that Sato-san had *already gone for a walk in the woods*. Though Ryu was reluctant to accept it, he realized his mentor and father figure was probably dead. Hearing that story, I was surprised to have seen the two of them talking in the club.

I barely recognized Ryu that morning. The loss of Sato-san was taking a toll on him. He looked haggard, like he had not slept well in days. In reality, it had been months. I felt sorry for him and decided we could talk about "us" later. I knew he would not be sad to delay that conversation.

"Let's rest a bit," I mumbled.

"Uh huh," he replied. Right then, my phone buzzed, indicating that I had a message. It was from Saphire. In all the excitement, I had forgotten her baby was due that week. My hands shook in anticipation, as I opened the email.

It was love at first sight! The face of that beautiful baby girl with dark brown eyes will remain in my heart forever. Diamond was still with her, and in love with the monk she was shagging. At the end of the message, Saphire told me she named her precious little daughter, Ruby. Her words filled me with hope of seeing them soon.

I sent a reply, telling her how thrilled I was for her and Takeshi, and told her that contacting me over the next few months was probably not a good idea. I did not want to involve my friends any more than necessary in my dangerous activities.

After writing down the important numbers, Ryu took my phone and destroyed it. He had already gotten rid of his car the night we went into hiding. He was paranoid that Damian would be able to find us through a tracking device. As much as I wanted to diminish his fears, I knew he was probably right.

PLAN Z

During the following week, the only person that we saw was Yuko. She was concerned about leaving us there, knowing the cabin belonged to a friend of Ryu's. I understood he was a monk. I thought it would be a funny coincidence if it turned out he was Diamond's boyfriend.

We anticipated Yuko's visits. Every day, she came with food, beverages and newspapers. I gave her a fat stack of bills for shopping and she bought us all kinds of Japanese delicacies. Some of the foods I liked and some did not strike my fancy. Ryu and Yuko loved to giggle at the expressions on my face when I tried foods I was eating for the first time.

Though we were enjoying ourselves, we had to face facts. We were on the run. Everything in my world changed that night at the Yamanashi club. Damian's buddies, who knew and respected Yuko's brother, asked her a few subtle questions because they remembered seeing us together, but she threw them off our trail.

I did not want Yuko getting involved with us, so I insisted that she stop coming to the cabin. As I watched her leave for the last time, it really tore me up inside. At least I knew her email address. We dreamed of seeing each other again soon. After she went away, I sat on the front porch by myself, contemplating life. I wanted to go home or flee to another destination, hide out in another country for a while.

When I suggested that we should catch a plane out, Ryu explained all the airports would be watched. Not only that, but Damian had spies who would be checking for any new airline bookings under our names. We were stuck in Japan.

We needed a plan, and not one for the faint of heart. Survival instinct kicked in again and a stronger version of me emerged. I sought an alternative to a life on the run from the mafia. We had to assume that Sato-san was dead. I had heard too many horror stories relating to the Japanese mafia. But Ryu loved him so much, and I doubted he could allow himself to accept the thought of Sato-san's demise.

As I consoled Ryu for his loss, I thought of my own family. I imagined my stepdad finishing the harvest on our farm. It was a special time of year for our family. During that period, we worked hard to get the crops cut, dried and collected. Throughout autumn, the bins would be filled with grain and our basement pantry would be stocked with all kinds of canned fruits and vegetables. We would be settling down, enjoying the prospect of a cozy, cold winter.

The nostalgic feeling was more than I could bear. For the first time, since being in Japan, I longed for my family and my country. I wanted to go home and was ashamed at how much I had taken for granted. All my life I had been rejecting the farm and its way of life. I had been yearning for the big city life, only to realize that there was no place like home. I hoped I would survive and be home for the birth of my niece.

The only thing keeping me in good spirits, besides Ryu's company were Yuko's visits, but she would not be coming back. I remembered her bringing her guitar and sitting on the tiny dilapidated back porch, jamming for me. It soothed me beyond words. On a few occasions, she brought her mobile recording studio so we would record ourselves. It was great to hear the songs we were composing.

I felt so motivated and inspired to create music with Yuko that spontaneous lyrics flew from me. Every night, I went to bed with a new melody in my head, a melody that needed to become a song. During the months I was in Tokyo, I had never been inspired the way I was in the mountains of Yamanashi.

In Roppongi, I never put myself in an environment that was conducive to composing music. In Yamanashi, it was my number one focus and my therapeutic outlet. Even though I was on the run and missed my family, I had found a measure of happiness.

During that creative period, The Crow came to my mind. From time to time, his cheerful face flashed in my memory and I recalled my vow to do something nice for him. Yuko and I wrote a rock inspired ballad on the guitar entitled, *The Crow*.

We wrote and recorded the song in one night and Yuko promised to send him an MP3 the next day. In the song, The Crow was a man who could change into a bird and escape to anywhere he wanted. The song was right up his alley and I pictured him rocking it out with his high-pitched voice.

I was also getting laid again. I do not know how many months I went without, but it was too long. Ryu and I were having bone rattling, orgasmic sessions, which left my ears ringing. I don't know why, but whenever I have particularly good sex, I can't hear properly for a while afterward. I was glad Yuko had the intuitiveness to buy condoms. I had no intention of getting pregnant while fleeing from gangsters.

The anger I felt toward Ryu had vanished, and I was thankful he did not contact me while he was on the run. He did not want to endanger me. Ryu was a man of few words. It seemed the more I tried to get him to open up, the more withdrawn he became. It was frustrating.

Before the incident at the club, I always prided myself in having a plan. Plans A, B and C were typical choices - sensible, though never dangerous. But I needed a Plan Z if I would ever have a normal life again, and I needed courage to pull it off.

While we were at the cabin, I hatched our Plan Z. It was our only escape. We had to take away the Damian threat. Just thinking about it unnerved me! Outnumbered and outgunned, we needed to outwit him.

The first part of my plan involved Ryu and I sneaking into Tokyo, hiding in the back of a rental car, driven by Yuko. Crystal and Amy had a rad place around the corner from my apartment in Azabu Juban. But we did not want to bring heat on them and we could not stay in my apartment. Crystale and Amy would rent us a hotel room and leave the key and address in their mailbox. We would pick it up and go directly to the room.

Crystale and Amy were forever hanging out at a spot called Sky Lounge. It was a club in Mori Tower, with an amazing view of the city from the fiftieth floor. All the beautiful and powerful people in Tokyo liked to be seen there, as it was a popular hangout for many, including Damian. As soon as he came into the club, the girls would contact us.

According to information that Yuko gathered, Damian was confident we could not escape Japan, and he guessed we had already gone back to Tokyo. I agonized with the last step of Plan Z. I wondered if I could kill him, if it actually came down to that.

I still had the gun I took the night of my encounter with Damian in the Yamanashi nightclub. It felt cold and heavy in my hand. It comforted and terrified me all at once, as it would determine my destiny.

A LIFE FOR A LIFE

I had died in my dreams many times in many different ways. I had been stabbed, drowned and mauled by a black panther. And with each dream, my death became more vivid and real to me. We had been in Tokyo for three days when the call came. It woke me from one of my mortal dreams, saving me from being hacked apart by a Samurai sword.

Startled from the dream, I leapt from the bed and answered the phone. I expected Crystale or Amy to be on the other end, telling me that Damian had showed up at the Sky Lounge. I wanted the nightmare to be over.

"I need to talk to you," said a timid voice.

"Crystale?" I barely recognized the voice on the other end.

"Yes. I need to come over right now," she said. Before I could ask her what was wrong, she hung up and I listened for a few seconds to the dial tone on the other end. It was a little before three in the afternoon and Ryu and I were still lounging in bed.

I was about to wake Ryu when suddenly a gouging pain ravaged my lower abdomen. It was more than a stomach ache and I struggled to catch my breath. It lasted for about a minute and then it was gone. I paused to recover and decided to throw a robe on so that I could accept our room service without flashing the hotel staff.

"Ryu, wake up." I nuzzled his neck as he turned toward me, blinking his eyes.

"Nani?" he asked, looking at me.

"Crystale is on her way over," I answered, trying to sound cheerful. He jumped out of bed and started dressing, nervous.

While waiting, I remembered a conversation that Ryu and I had days earlier. I was curious to know what his role with the mafia was and I finally asked him, straight up. After one of his famous long pauses he finally looked away and answered, "I can't tell you, but I've done bad things."

Our plan was for a three-way standoff with Damian at the Sky Lounge. When Damian was partying with his girls, he left his bodyguards downstairs. If Ryu and I could sneak by unnoticed up to the lounge with our guns, we would have a definite advantage and we could offer *a life for a life*. Caught in the crossfire between both of us, pointing loaded weapons, Damian would have to decide how much he was willing to sacrifice for revenge. But Damian was unpredictable and we resolved that one of us would have to kill him, if necessary.

Just then someone knocked on the door. I was surprised that my friend had gotten there so fast. Ryu grabbed his gun from the bedside table where he kept it and gestured for me to check the peephole.

"Calm down. It's just Crystale," I tried to reassure him. He remained tense and ready to spring into action. I looked through the peephole and sighed when I saw Crystale, standing with her hands crossed on the other side of the door.

Crystale slipped through the door and just as I was about to close it, a big black shoe stopped it. A huge, powerful hand reached through and tried to grab me. I stumbled back, crashing into a table and crawling as I fumbled for the gun that had been knocked to the floor.

When Damian kicked the door wide open and stepped inside, his gun was drawn and locked on me. We heard a distinctive click and looked over to see Ryu, whose gun was pointed at Damian's face.

"Drop it, Ryu!" Damian shouted, "Or I swear I will kill this bitch!" Crystale cringed in a corner of the room, crying, her hands covering her ears. Finally clutching the gun in my hands, I stood, pointing the barrel toward a man I despised.

"I'm ready to die, Damian," I sneered. "So *kill* me, if you've got the balls, because you know Ryu will blow your face off."

"You have exactly one minute," Ryu insisted, "to decide what you're going to do, because I *am* going to kill you!"

"Wait!" Damian yelled, attempting to smile. "We don't have to do this. What do you want?"

"I'm going to kill you," Ryu insisted. "I blame you for what happened to Sato-san."

"What happened to Sato-san had nothing to do with me, Ryu. I was following orders," Damian almost pleaded. "You of all people should understand that. You know how this all works." He paused, looking toward me. "Of *course* you don't want me to shoot her. You're in love with each other – so pathetic! And I'm not ready to die today."

"I'm tired of running, Damian," I said. "Either way, I'm done."

"What's it going to be, Ryu," he continued. "What do you want?"

Ryu paused, contemplating, no expression. "What's it going to take, Ryu? What's it going to take for me to walk away from this?"

"Safe passage out of Tokyo, for the both of us," Ryu spoke, closing on Damian.

"*She* is free to go. You have my word and my boss' word that no one will touch her," Damian conceded. "But you are a different matter. With you, its business, and you're a loose end."

"I'd rather be *dead* than without you!" I insisted to Ryu, drawing my shaking gun to a place inches from Damian's forehead. "Shoot that bastard now! Or I *will*!"

"Now hold on, both of you!" Damian countered, raising his hands. "Let's not lose our minds. I know we can work something out."

"The both of us, or you die," Ryu said, barely speaking.

"I can't do that. You know I can't do that," Damian repeated. "My boss would kill me for letting you go, but I have a compromise."

"I'm listening," Ryu nodded.

"Okay, she goes. We'll even pay her way if we have to. And you – we were brothers once. We were best friends," Damian ventured. "Based on our history, I owe you some consideration. Here is my proposal: she goes free, and you – I will give you a two hour head start, and then I'll come after you with everything I've got. That way, if you're smart and lucky, at least you'll have a chance."

"Ryu, I don't trust him," I interrupted.

"Call your boss, Damian," Ryu insisted. "I want to hear from him on his honor that she'll be free to go, and then we have a deal."

"No!" I protested. "I won't go without you. We have to be together!"

The phone call was brief and to the point. Sufficiently assured that I would be safe, Ryu began to name additional conditions, but all at once, the room started to sway. I rocked hard to the right and was thrown to the floor and when I looked around I realized that it was the entire room that was moving.

I had felt a couple of earthquakes in my life, but nothing could have prepared me for the intensity of that one. Being forty floors up only increased the earthquake's force, as people and chairs were knocked to the ground. Ryu and Damian were on the floor in a heap, but I could not tell if they were wrestling with each other or struggling to stand. I did not think it could get any worse, but it did. And for the second time in that evening, but for different reasons, I was certain I was going to die.

I glanced out the window and saw the tallest buildings in Tokyo, swaying back and forth. The thought of those skyscrapers crashing down was a terrifying thought. As I watched in shocked silence, I felt another horrible pain tear through me. It felt like a severe menstrual cramp and I was overcome with blinding pain as I closed my eyes to it. But before I could compose myself, the mysterious pain became unbearable and the world went dark.

MARCH 11

I woke up at Crystale and Amy's apartment and discovered that they had rescued me. When I first saw Damian at my door, I had thought Crystale had betrayed me. But she had only given information that he would have found out sooner or later and if she hadn't she would be dead right then. I didn't have any hard feelings against her. On the contrary, I was apologetic that I had involved them in my dangerous dealings.

Crystale told me of the events following my loss of consciousness. When the earthquake started, she was flung to the floor, where she sheltered under a table for safety. She heard a gunshot, and then she heard two more. Terrified, she peeked out when she thought the danger had passed. Ryu and Damian were nowhere to be found, but there were bullet holes in the walls and a trail of blood leading out of the room.

I was desperate to find out what happened to Ryu and if he was okay, but there was no way to reach him. I wondered why he had run out of the hotel room. Little did I know that the whole country was in chaos after experiencing Japan's most devastating earthquake, the fourth largest in recorded history.

I lied in the bed Crystale and Amy shared, with a fluffy fuchsia blanket covering me all the way up to my chin. I felt hopeless, but I could not begin to express my fear to them. I had thought life could not get any worse when we were running from the mafia, but a life without Ryu seemed unthinkable.

Before we returned to Tokyo to attempt Plan Z, Ryu had taken me to a Japanese temple.

"Where are we, Ryu?" I asked, as we stopped next to a beautiful wooden building. Yuko had driven us there. The impeccably maintained gardens surrounded us and stretched on as far as the eye could see. They smelled fabulous through my open window.

"A sacred place, a temple," he answered in a quiet voice. He stayed inside the car and stared straight ahead for a few minutes. Then he turned his face toward me, watching. As he took my hand, all I could think of was how lucky I was. He looked deep into my eyes, and I felt his emotions without having to speak. He was trying to communicate what did not need to be said.

We needed to pray for our safety and for the plan we concocted, since it was crazy and we both knew it. Language was a barrier, but we spoke the language of our hearts. When we were together, we did not need to talk. One look or breath was all it took for us to share volumes.

When we got out of the car and started walking the temple grounds, there was not another soul around. We walked for hours in silence among the tiny ornamental maple trees on miniature stone pathways. The cherry trees were beginning to bud and the promise of pretty blossoms kept us admiring the mountain forests for hours.

When the sun began to set, we retreated to the temple. There was a vast structure before us that I realized was an entryway. It looked like a giant doorway and as I walked through it, I felt the power of the monument vibrate throughout my body. Before another sacred building, we bowed in unison and clapped our hands. I knew that we were both thinking the same thing: "Keep us safe. Let this all work out."

Just as we were about to leave, a little old man came out of a house, obscured by trees. He was wearing a long black robe, tied at the waist. Friendly, he spoke to Ryu in Japanese, as if they had known each other a long time. At the end of their conversation, he turned to me and shook my hand, saying in perfect English, "Won't you please come into my home and have some refreshments?"

"Thank you for your graciousness," I answered, surprised at how excellent his English was. "We would be delighted to join you."

He seemed ecstatic to be practicing English. We took off our shoes as we entered his house, which was a gorgeous example of an old-style Japanese dwelling. There was a ledge at the entrance for shoes. From there, we stepped up into his beautiful home.

The old man showed us to a large table, which was low and had cushions all along, for seating. After we all sat down, his wife came in, wearing a dark robe similar to her husband's. She did not sit down and join us. Rather, she bowed low and offered us tea.

I knew all Japanese women were not subservient, having heard about the wrath of more than one wife in Roppongi. I wondered what her interests were and wished she had joined us and told her stories.

"Can you join us?" I heard myself asking, before I thought about it. She seemed shocked, though pleased, and she took a seat near me.

"What's your name?" I asked, and before I could ask her in Japanese, she answered in a clear, confident voice. "Fuji." Her English was just as good as her husband's.

Ryu and I sat and heard many of their stories as we relaxed with them that afternoon. We had a good time. We got what we came for that day, a simple and blessed afternoon. As we were about to leave, Fuji showed me a picture of her son and daughter-in-law. I hardly recognized the vivacious, dark-haired girl in the picture as Diamond, but there she was, as clear as day. She seemed a different woman as she gazed at her wicked monk in adoration.

Ryu recognized her as he gazed at the picture with a smile on his face. We looked at each other and grinned, but we did not say anything to our new friends. We did not want anyone else becoming involved with our drama. We were just pleased knowing Diamond would be safe and happy in such a sacred place.

I had not told a soul about the things I had been through, but as I sat there with Amy and Crystale, I felt an overwhelming need to unburden myself. I trusted those women. And it was not every day that someone saved your life.

Before I could even begin to form a sentence, Amy was at bedside with a wide-eyed, worried look on her face. Her brow wrinkled as she blurted out, "I don't want to panic you even more, but you need to know. Your apartment's been burned down."

The odds tacked against me were beginning to weigh me down. It did not make sense, but instead of being hysterical, I was elated. Yet the happiness I felt had nothing to do with the fact that my belongings and money were probably gone.

There was more to it. The pains I had been feeling began to make sense. I had not felt them since I woke up, but I realized what caused them. *They were labor pains!* I was feeling sympathy pains for my twin. She must have been giving birth to her baby!

I asked Amy if I could use her phone, but she said it would be impossible to reach anyone in Canada. After the earthquake, the phone lines were tied up with millions of people calling at the same time. The girls did not have a computer, so Skype was out of the question. I wondered how my sister was and I wished I was with her.

The pains were not the sharp side pains I imagined, but deep menstrual pains, which lasted for longer than I thought I could bear. After I had awakened, the pains I felt were replaced by euphoria, encompassing my entire being. But it was mixed with the overwhelming grief I was feeling from losing Ryu.

The room started to sway and I became nauseous, realizing we were in for another large aftershock. We looked at each other, petrified with fear, not knowing if we would survive the next one.

I remembered the last night that Ryu and I lied together on our futon. Our Yamanashi hideaway was quiet in the last few days. Neither of us wanted to talk about the future. I had to ask. As I stroked his ears the way he liked, I whispered softly into his neck, "Where is a safe place to meet if things go bad?"

We did not want to jinx our plan with this kind of talk, but we knew there were huge risks in our plan. Ryu's muscles tensed as he sighed, thinking about the question. Confident, he answered, as if he had been waiting to have this discussion for a while.

"If things get bad, I will find you," he answered as he lit up a half-dube that was in the ashtray. Smoke swirling around him, he exhaled before continuing, not knowing how ultimately fine he looked. The sexiest guys are the ones who don't even know it.

"I want to go back to Canada," I interrupted. He still had not answered my question about where we could meet, and I could not think of a logical choice.

"I know, Rose," he answered in the same confident tone.

I wanted to see my family. I missed them, but did not want to put my family and friends in potential danger. A selfish part of me wished that I had not maced that room. I should have gone back to Canada before I got so greedy. But I had chosen true love and I refused any regret.

I had to accept my life on the run would not be ending anytime soon. I would not jeopardize the safety and happiness of my family by returning to them with murderers following me. But isolation from my twin and my family was devastating to me. My heart was broken.

"We meet in Thailand if something happen. We meet at before resort," Ryu said. I just nodded, trying hard to hold back my tears, not looking at him. His soft hand caressed my chin as he lifted my tear filled eyes toward his own. Amy's wide blue eyes brought me back from the memory of Ryu as I steeled myself for yet another twist in my life story, spiraling out of control.

"How do you know my apartment got burned down?" I asked, monitoring the ever increasing vibrations that shook the room. I thought the aftershocks were getting bigger.

"We went by to talk to you the other day," Amy explained, "and the front door of your apartment was wide open. So we decided to go in and surprise you. But for some reason, we got the major creeps..."

"I mean, the hairs on the back of my neck started to stand up," Crystale continued. "And I was like, 'Let's get out of here, Amy! This is weird!'"

"But, I was like, 'No way, Crystale! What if something happened to Rose?'" Amy interrupted. "So we went in, even though we were freaked out of our minds!"

"We were almost in your apartment," Crystale whispered, "when we saw an enormous, scary looking dude, rifling through the papers on your desk. We froze in utter terror for a second, not knowing what to do."

"Then," Amy said, miming their movements, "when he turned to the side, we saw it was Damian! I don't know how we got out of there without him seeing us, but I have never been so scared in my life." "We went by the outside of your building the next day and saw your apartment had been totally burned out," Amy sighed, in tears.

I did not care. The loss of the money and material possessions were the least of my concerns. All that mattered was my family, my safety and the love I felt. I would have given the world to be with Ryu, my friends and family when the nightmare was over.

I did not tell the girls I had a flight booked to leave for Thailand the next morning.

"Let's turn on the news," I decided. I needed to get a feel for stories regarding the after-effects of the earthquake.

Usually, we avoided television like the plague. There was only one English speaking channel, but it lingered on dreary and depressing world news. The Japanese stations hosted strange, absurd game shows. Contestants made fools of themselves, while over-the-top audience members covered their mouths, exclaiming "Ehhhhhh!"

When we turned on the television that day, however, all the news anchors, women and men, wore hardhats. It was a wake-up call, reminding us how much the earthquake had affected Japan. We were overwhelmed with images that belonged in *Godzilla* and other disaster films. An enormous black wave of destructive sand and debris wiped out coastal communities, forever changing the lives of elderly populations. It was the first tsunami I had ever witnessed and it was terrifying, even on video.

We watched Japan's worst nightmare play before our eyes. On one channel, we saw a vast, watery vortex form, sucking in people, cars and homes. In other footage, people atop of buildings, waving white sheets were trying to be seen and rescued. The death toll appeared in the top right-hand corner of the screen, with casualties climbing quickly.

I thought I had seen the worst Japan had to offer, but events had gotten much worse. As the evening continued, the three of us huddled on the bed and cuddled under the blanket. We heard they might be having trouble with nuclear reactors in northeastern Japan. We began to panic. The situation was being compared to Chernobyl.

My mother always warned me of the dangers of nuclear power, but I never really believed it would have an effect on my life. The reality was I stood before a possible nuclear holocaust and my visa was about to expire. The universe was telling me to get out.

I hoped I would not be followed. I was scheduled to leave to Thailand in the morning, but from what I saw on the news, every subway was shut down and every taxi was occupied. People were stranded all over the city. Hotels and coffee shops were packed. Bicycle shops were sold out. Transportation was a major problem.

I thought of my friends as I fingered the cat figurine around my neck. Svetlana was intuitive. Her advice had always been simple: follow your heart. I had faith that Ryu was still alive.

Without it, I would not have been strong enough to continue. As usual, I already had a plan. I knew what I needed to do.

EARTHQUAKE AFTERMATH

Crystale, Amy and I tried to sleep, because we knew we would need our strength for the next day. But I did not sleep well, sandwiched between two terrified girls, suffering through night tremors. It reminded me of trying to jump in bed with my twin when I was scared, as a little girl.

"Where do you think he is?" Amy asked, out of the blue. We had been talking about Ryu for hours, and it was driving me insane.

"I don't want to talk about it anymore," I snapped. Thinking about Ryu made me worry all the more.

The girls thought I should call the hospitals, but I did not see the point because the lines would be busy and Ryu would never go to a hospital anyway unless... *No! I did not want to think about it!*

"Sorry girls," I rued, "I'm not myself right now." And I *was* sorry for my harsh words. They were loyal friends, and I did not know where I would be without them.

"Don't worry, Rose. You've been through so much," Amy comforted, stroking my hair. We had decided to catch the next plane back to Canada.

While I already had my ticket to Thailand, I was going to wait around to see if Ryu would make the flight. I figured he would be a no-show. With all the commotion going on in Japan after the earthquake, I imagined I would be low on the Japanese mafia's list of concerns.

I was still at the airport, waiting for Ryu. The flight to Thailand came and left with neither of us on it. Amy, Crystale and I booked the next flight back to Vancouver, with mixed feelings. Boarding the plane back to Canada was surreal and uncomfortable for me. There were many long faces on the plane, many who were thinking of loved ones left behind.

I thought of Saphire, Takeshi and their baby girl, Ruby. They lived in a small Northern community with Takeshi's family. We had no way of knowing what happened to them during the earthquake. We tried to Facebook all our friends when we were at the airport, but with no responses. I hoped Diamond and her hunky monk were safe. I did not mean to leave without saying goodbye.

As we lifted off, I said a prayer to all the people in Japan who were homeless or without food or warmth because of the quake. And worse, some had lost loved ones, homes and businesses. On that night, even the babies were silent as we flew over Japan, headed west over the vast, churning waters of the Pacific Ocean.

BACK HOME

July 1 – I had been back in Canada for only three months, but I was still alive. The Yaks (*Yakuza*) had not come in the middle of the night to break in and drag me from bed, kicking and screaming. They had not been at the airport, as I feared. I still had nightmares about them though. Ryu still had not contacted me.

I expected an email letting me know that he was okay, if he was. But day after diligent day, I checked my emails and for naught. Yet I still refused to believe he was dead. I was hoping that Ryu had not suffered the same fate as Sato-san, although we never actually found out what happened to him. We just assumed he was dead. I clung to the hope that Ryu was alive and that hope sustained me.

Night after night, I dreamt of Ryu, until finally I decided to control the dream... I created a doorway in the wall and willed it to open. It did. I thought to myself, *if I could make the door open, I might be able to make someone appear in the entryway*. Immediately Ryu appeared and we embraced. I felt close to him, but I knew that it was only a facade. I woke up the next morning with an aching, frustrating need for him that grew daily.

While lying in bed I tried to control my dreams, but my untrained mind spun out of control and often left me smack dab in the middle of a gruesome nightmare. I did not know which was worse, the nightmares or the waiting, or not knowing what had really become of Ryu. One night, I had a dream that surprised me. It was the dream where Ryu and I leapt off the cliff together, laughing all the way down. I did not want to get my hopes up, but I prayed the dream was a good omen.

I was still in bed when my twin, Daisy, barged into my room with her three month old daughter, Melody, in her arms.

"Happy Cannabis Day!"

Daisy yanked the blankets from my face and thrust her baby into my arms. "I need to pee. Hold her." And with that, she ran to the bathroom, leaving me alone with my niece. As I held her, I marveled at her beauty. She made me understand pure, unconditional love. Her trusting new eyes studied me. Daisy forgave me for not being there during childbirth, but going forward, I would be there for Melody and her.

When I first returned to Canada, I did not stay with family members and tried to keep a low profile. However, after a month of hiding out, cabin fever drove me from living in fear. I wanted to see my sister and niece on a more regular basis, so I moved in with them.

****

Japan was still in the middle of a catastrophe that some likened to a third atomic bomb. No one planned for an earthquake of such magnitude, but they sure as hell *should* have. It did not make sense that a government, whose policy was to take care of its citizens, would sanction nuclear energy, which historically had proven deadly not only in Japan, but all over the world.

I knew that most of the residents who lived around the stricken Fukushima plants did not want any part of its reactors. Many who spoke on television in the aftermath had no idea the power they were using to light their houses was coming from nuclear reactors. I had no idea. The long term effects of the nuclear contamination were yet to be realized.

****

Baby Melody's gurgling and drooling all over my chest distracted me from my reflections. I was charmed by her little smile as I started to play peek-a-boo with her. The smile left my face when I caught a whiff of a rank baby fart. No problem. I was getting good at changing diapers.

"Let's check that. Whew! Okay, time for the change table." I began singing a diaper changing song as I carried her to the room.

The room was nicely decorated. Daisy and I painted it a light lilac color and hung white letters, spelling out Melody's name. A tiny, white armoire sat to one side, and I opened a drawer and found a cute little outfit.

"Do you like this outfit, Melody?" I asked. She gurgled again, smiling with a toothless mouth. I finished changing the mustard-colored diaper and dressed her in tiny clothing. I had spent the last of my money redecorating Melody's room. I thought my money would have lasted longer than three months, but there I was, flat broke again. When I got back to Vancouver, I had thirty-five thousand dollars in my bank account.

But upon arrival, I had signed myself up to study at a recording arts program that started after summer. The program cost me more than fifteen thousand dollars. Then I rented a three bedroom apartment for Daisy, Melody and myself and pre-paid the rent for a year, which ended up being about fifteen thousand dollars.

That left me with five thousand dollars. I needed a new laptop and recording equipment. I was stoked that I would have the knowledge and means to create songs and music files that everyone could hear. It was a beautiful power.

After a final shopping spree at Pottery Barn Kids for Melody's room, I was broke again. And with the money went the stress that came with earning and keeping it. I traveled across the world to Japan to make money. And what had the adventure provided me? A broken heart and the constant fear of being captured!

****

I did not regret my decision to travel to Japan. In doing so, I found myself. Like so many others, I started my journey convinced that having money would make everything better. I finally understood that even with little or no possessions, the only thing I needed to be happy was a dream and family love. Of course I missed Ryu, but I had found peace within, at last.

And my relationship with my new niece was good for me. I hugged her and kissed her forehead as Melody tried to squirm from my grasp. She was already a willful little girl. "You're going to meet a little friend today!" I whispered in an excited voice.

Saphire, her baby, Ruby, and her husband, Takeshi, were flying in that morning. I could not believe that I was going to see her again. One night, a couple of weeks after I returned, I had a dream that all my friends came to see me. The fantasy had been playing out in my daydreams since leaving Japan, but that dream was so vivid that when I awoke, I had tears streaming down my face.

I missed Svetlana more each day. I wanted to contact her, Lula, Amy and Crystale. I wondered about Yuko as well, if she had been exposed to caesium and radiation levels. While I was in hiding, I was not in contact with Saphire or Diamond.

I was holed up in a hotel room outside Vancouver, trying to lay low. I closed my Facebook account, just in case the Japanese mafia was still after me. I opened another account under a new name and contacted people after I was out of danger.

One night, I wrote an email to all my girlfriends. I asked them to come to Canada for a reunion. I proposed Cannabis Day/Canada Day as a good day for everyone to fly in, if they could make it. In Vancouver, any day associated with enjoying the "green" was quite the celebration.

Email responses poured in. My friends were happy that I had finally made contact. They were afraid for me during the earthquake. Svetlana emailed first, telling me she had booked a flight and could not wait to see me. Her business was doing great. My email was perfectly timed, as she had been planning to vacation.

Amy and Crystale emailed next, telling me they were in Miami working as topless waitresses on a party yacht. They would be back in time for the summer reunion, but they were having the time of their lives. They said they had Latino lovers, who were brothers, and that it would be hard to tear themselves from the romance and nightclubs.

When Yuko emailed, it was short and to the point. She let me know that she would be coming to Vancouver and that she was fine. She was anticipating meeting a cute Canadian guy and performing shows.

I could not believe my luck when Saphire emailed and told me she could make it with her baby and hubby. She said Diamond could not come because she was doing charity work in Japan to help the Fukushima disaster survivors.

I waited for an email from Lula, but it never came. Finally, I asked Svetlana if she could track her down in Estonia. Svetlana had friends all over Europe, so I was not even surprised one night when she emailed me, telling me that she had gotten to the bottom of the mystery.

Lula's mom had died. I remembered stories she had told about her mother, and they had been so full of happiness and light. They were very close. I could not begin to imagine how she felt losing her.

In the throes of depression, Lula met a man who stole her heart. But with her heart, he also stole her house, respect and sense of pride. When she married him, he became part owner of her beloved house. One cold, blustery night, he forced her sister to move out into the streets. Lula hated herself for not having the courage to stop him. But he beat her so badly that she had to leave in order to remain alive. She spent a month in a hospital, recovering from a concussion.

When she was released, she knew what she had to do. She found an agent and signed another contract to work as a hostess in Japan. Lula, who hated the industry more than any of us and found it harder to endure the routine, was going back to it.

But before she had a chance to return, her abusive husband saw to it that nobody would ever again experience the pleasure of his wife's company. At home with a rifle, he put a bullet through her brain before taking his own life. When Svetlana told me Lula was gone, I was devastated. A part of me died with her, knowing I would never see her again. Lula was too young to die.

I was in mourning when I got an email from Saphire, telling me she had just watched The Crow on a Japanese talk show. Attached was a link to a funny YouTube clip of him, belting out a song that Yuko and I composed. His interpretation and expressions were comical.

He wore a purple cape, tights and a long fake beard as he jumped around like a man on fire. He danced and flung his hands around spastically, bringing the audience including the host to hysterics. Only in Japan could such a random and weird performance turn someone into an overnight star.

Our reunion date came quicker than I anticipated. I spent the week picking up girls from the airport. Yuko used whatever savings she had to fly in first. When she arrived, we ran at each other and embraced. She wanted to make the most of her first time in North America.

Svetlana flew in soon after, a fresh reminder of Europe. She was confident and focused. Her art gallery was doing well, while she was gaining notoriety as a painter. Thousands of kilometers away from Japan, things had not changed between us.

All the girls would be staying in our cramped apartment, like the old days. We did not see it as an inconvenience. On the contrary, we were excited to see what kind of mischief we could get into together.

WRECK BEACH

I was staring at the most massive shlong I had ever seen, not directly though. That would have been rude. *How did I always find this kind of sick entertainment wherever in the world I went?* I thought as I took my sunglasses off to wipe them. The sunglasses were to protect my eyes from the sun and to protect naked people from my wandering eyes.

While at a nude beach, we did as the Romans did or something like that. The bubbly in our plastic beach glasses was impairing my ability to recite quotes. It was the first time I was drunk in the three months I had been back in Canada. I had an occasional glass of wine or preferably champagne at dinner, but I was making a point to slow down my drinking.

I did not want to address it, even internally. I had been relying on booze far too much. It was a good thing that hooch was less accessible in Canada. Almost every convenience store in Japan sold it and there was a convenience store on every other block. The stores were everywhere and it was sometimes hard for me to walk by without getting lured in by them. I felt the urge to buy a *chu-hai* (canned *shochu* cocktail) and chug it as I walked down the street, just because I could get away with it.

It was not just my addiction and the daily struggle with it that scared me. I was afraid I would end up run down, flabby and diabetes ridden, like many of the custies in clubs, who had poured too many bottles down their throats. I valued my health and beauty.

Alcoholism hit too close to home for me. My granny lived on the streets for many years and as a result of discrimination and vice, she spent time behind bars. She and my grandfather succumbed to heroin addictions, but they never lost sense of their humor and their commitment to love and integrity.

Throughout Vancouver, homelessness and addiction was present, regardless of age, race or sex. It was a tough life on the cold and bitter streets of the downtown Eastside of Vancouver. I always kept spare change or a smile for those people. They needed my kindness and empathy rather than judgement or pity. In their eyes I saw my grandparents.

****

We ventured four hundred crude steps down the Wreck Beach stairs. Nobody complained as we descended in a single-file line. I had brought my boom-bag, which was useful because it played music and carried stuff at the same time. I felt like a mule, because I had a baby strapped to the front of me as I led the huge procession down the stairs.

They were in for a surprise. Wreck beach was not only a nude beach, but a party beach. There were bongo circles, people selling Jell-O shooters, naked women covered in sparkles blowing bubbles and men wearing only fanny packs and socks, selling ganja and beer. It was a gorgeous day, with a slight breeze that ruffled our hair as we stopped at the end of the stairs.

I surveyed the group, grinning. There was Diamond (who had decided to come anyway) and Saphire, who came with their men and Saphire's baby, Ruby, who I already loved. They stood side-by-side, men flanking them, one carrying a baby. Yuko stood next to Svetlana, the two in conversation. I was not surprised they became fast friends. Daisy led the way into the crowd, searching out a good area to put our blankets down.

Tiffany and Justin did not attend because they were busy with their new bar, but they sent their love and promised to come to the next event. Amy and Crystale called to say they would not make it after all because both had become engaged in Miami.

Some people would think I was crazy, considering my choice to become a hostess in Japan and all the crazy things that had happened while I was there, but I had grown. I had become a woman in Japan.

Melody stared at her hands like she had never seen them before. The sunlight reflecting on them sparkled on her new skin. Her nails were covered with protective mittens so she would not scratch her face.

She would never be a hostess. It was not her path, and I was grateful for that.

The foreign hostess market was already on its way out when I arrived. I saw its demise. The industry was no longer profitable, unless hostesses could find Sugar Daddies. Even before the earthquake, the best customers were the older men, who drank and partied and worked their asses off, knowing they would not last much longer. Younger men were not profitable. As the older generation died off, so would the hostess industry.

****

That morning, I checked my bank account online the way that I had countless times before in the days of Tom. I assumed there was only $66.42 left in the account. When I discovered I had an extra three thousand dollars in the account, my heart soared.

Upon investigating, I found out that the money had come from The Crow, for royalties on the song that Yuko and I wrote for him. I received a letter from The Crow a few days later. He told me he was touched by the song and that he and his twin boys would be traveling overseas soon. I was ecstatic.

****

I was in love with a country and people. I admired the fact that they were able to maintain their culture through so much adversity. The people remained steadfast and were proud of their heritage and ancestry.

My senses would never be the same after sampling the Japanese cuisine, men, art and music. I would never truly understand the culture of Japan, but that wouldn't stop me from trying. I felt like an explorer.

I had learned to bow in Japan, but I would never learn to bow down and be silent about things that I didn't agree with. Besides, society needed people like me to shake things up a bit.

I did not agree with the roles women were expected to play in Japanese society. I believed those expectations sometimes robbed girls of the right to be individuals. I cringed every time I saw how highly subservient behavior was revered among the men, who controlled Japanese society and dictated the behavior of its women.

Yuko was an exception to the rule. Of course, there were so many like her. But even with her I sensed a degree of unhappiness. She wasn't very close to her family because they were always nagging at her to get married. She was already in her mid-thirties, though she appeared much younger. Her family was unhappy that she was still unmarried, had tattoos, was an outspoken musician and refused to conform. I loved her all the more for it, but I think her nonconformity resulted in a sort of darkness about her.

I never understood why people in Japan accepted the conditions of the "live-in-divorces" that they imposed upon themselves. They would rather live unhappy lives rather than divorcing in shame.

I disliked some of the traditional Japanese customs, but I knew I was ignorant about the complicated spirit of Japan and its people. Ryu had told me that understanding Japan meant I would need to know about *Bushido*, or the way of the warrior. He told me that every Japanese person still possessed that feeling deep inside them.

I had never felt like a warrior. I went to Japan in search of independence and wealth, and I found love, knowledge and friendship. But I also found a warrior I did not know existed in me. I survived an earthquake, trouble with the mafia and a career in a red-light district. But instead of feeling jaded, I felt grateful for my small place in the world and the uncomplicated happiness of life.

Ultimately, being a Tokyo hostess taught me that I did not have to fear what others thought about me. Before coming to Japan, I was weighed down trying to be society's ideal version of a successful woman, instead of simply being me.

My experience freed me from a burden that ran deeper than I had ever imagined. I gave thanks for my beautiful, inspiring time in Japan and for all the wonderful people I had met along the way.

I felt vibrant, full of energy and ready for whatever life had in store for me. I had begun studying Japanese at a language school three times a week and I was starting to see a big difference. I wanted to be able to tell Ryu that I loved him in his own language when or if I finally saw him again.

****

When we settled down onto our blankets, the boys started up a game of Frisbee and we sat on the blanket, sipping chilled drinks and playing with babies.

All of a sudden, Diamond sat up straight, stiff as a board. She craned her neck, looking over my shoulder as she slipped the sunglasses down her nose. Gawking, her eyes bulged out and she began to splutter, "Rose! You would never believe! Look!"

In a trance, I turned to see Ryu, walking down the sand toward us with familiar strides. I had told him about my yearly Cannabis Day celebration on Wreck Beach, but I never expected that he would actually show up!

He was shirtless, tanned and brawnier than I remembered, with a shining golden figurine hanging from his neck, but it was definitely Ryu. Even in the distance, I could see his dragon tattoo. But I also spotted a short, jagged scar, snaking around his heart.

I rose to my feet and took a deep breath before I approached him, grinning ear to ear. I knew he would come.

AKNOWLEDGEMENTS

When I began writing this book it was as a daily or weekly journal. It was a way for me to create a physical art form from my time in Japan. It soon became an outlet for me to tell the truth about the Japanese hostess industry.

Writing the Roppongi story became an addiction. I would rush home every night and giggle away in glee at the honest, colorful stories, or sometimes cry at their sadness and tragedy.

I did not hold back at telling this tale, though society would have me keep silent. Many of the friends that I met look back on their experiences thankfully, with fondness. But to others, the time that we spent should remain hidden, filled with stigma and shame.

The negative reactions expressed and the ignorance that most people have towards the hostess industry made me want to write this book even more, to show the human and humorous side to the women, customers and staff of Roppongi.

To all the people that helped and inspired me to write this book, thank you a million times over. I could not have done it without you.

I wish to give my never ending gratitude to all the loving family I met in Roppongi. You know who you are.

Thanks to The Creator for all the beauty and intrigue of life.

I am forever grateful to my mother, Arlette Alcock for her wisdom and strength and to my grandmother Roseline Brabant.

To my husband Tetsuo and my little girl, Riena, you are the light in my life. Thanks for teaching me daily the true meaning of patience and love.

Thanks to my sister Belle and her wonderful husband Vincent for your positive energy and constructive criticism.

Thanks to all my other family love including all three dads, my two bros and their wives and my niece, Eden who stayed up late with me helping with small, tedious details. I love you.

Thanks to Bridget Ruth Kelly and all the other anonymous photographers who submitted photos.

And last, but definitely not least, thanks to Caprice De Luca, Marcus McGee and Tricia Lee at Pegasus Books for your professionalism, creativity and positivity throughout this entire process.

Rose Beach

Champagne Salary: Diary of a Tokyo Hostess

Photography: Euvie Ivanova
Visual Art: F.alt Photographics
Make Up Artist: Andrea Tiller
Cover Model: Sarah Marvin
Cover Layout: Tricia Lee